SKARA HOUSE

AT THE MEDIAEVAL UNIVERSITY OF PARIS.

HISTORY, TOPOGRAPHY, AND CHARTULARY

WITH RESUMES IN FRENCH AND SWEDISH

TEXTS AND STUDIES
IN THE HISTORY OF MEDIAEVAL EDUCATION

EDITED BY **A. L. GABRIEL** AND **J. N. GARVIN**

N⁰ IX

ASTRIK L. GABRIEL
Director of the Mediaeval Institute
University of Notre Dame

Skara House
at the Mediaeval University of Paris.
History, Topography, and Chartulary

WITH RESUMES IN FRENCH AND SWEDISH

1 9 6 0
THE   MEDIAEVAL   INSTITUTE
UNIVERSITY OF NOTRE DAME

NOTRE DAME, INDIANA U. S. A.

To Trudie and Wallace Bedolfe

TABLE OF CONTENTS

LIST OF PLATES

PREFACE

At the present time, when there is so much talk about international relations and such great emphasis upon intellectual cooperation and cultural relations among the various countries, we are easily inclined to lower the « iron curtain » of *Ignoramus* upon the achievements that were accomplished in this field by the universities of the Christian Middle Ages with their humble scholars, masters, and students.

In addition to high ranking ecclesiastics, such as popes, cardinals, and bishops, the mediaeval Cathedral Chapters, the *capitulum canonicorum*, also shared the important tasks of promoting studies at foreign universities and helping scholars from their dioceses, who were migrating from one center of studies to another. The Cathedral Chapter was composed of many canons, frequently alumni of foreign universities. There was always one to raise his voice in the *capitulum*, requesting the sending of a worthy representative of his diocese to his former *studium*. Generous financial contributions usually accompanied such a proposal.

Among such Cathedral Chapters, the members of the Skara Cathedral Chapter, the *Capitulum Ecclesiae Sanctae Mariae Scarensis*, played a considerable role in promoting French-Swedish cultural and intellectual relations.

It is the aim of this study 1) to shed light upon the efforts made for Skara House by the illustrious members of the Chapter, all former students of the University of Paris; 2) to give new information on the topography of Skara House, located in Clos-Bruneau; 3) to analyze and publish the extant unedited documents relating to the purchase, upkeep, and renting of this House, which was called *Hotel de Suesse* and later House of *Notre-Dame* after the patron saint of the Chapter of Skara.

It is my pleasant duty to express my gratitude to the Rev. Dr. Joseph N. Garvin, C. S. C. for his most valuable suggestions. His

11

great talent for editorial work lightened my task beyond measure. Turning to Sweden, I wish to thank Dr. Olaf Jägersköld, the Director of *Riksarkivet*, Dr. Carl Nordenfalk, Director of the Nationalmuseum, Dr. Åke Sällström, Dr. Svante Hallberg in Stockholm and conservator in *Riksarkivet*, and Dr. Folke Nordström at the University of Upsala for their most appreciated assistance during my research in the archives and cities of Lund, Skara, Upsala, and Stockholm.

In *Douce France*, I am most grateful to Mr. Germain Calmette, Conservateur en chef of the Library of the University of Paris, to Mademoiselle Yvonne Lanhers, Madame Agnes Hosotte-Reynaud and Mr. Bernard Mahieu, Conservateurs in the *Archives Nationales*, to Madame Madeleine Laurain-Portemer in the *Bibliothèque Nationale*, who facilitated my access to the original documents in every way. In the *Institut de Recherches et d'Histoire des Textes*, Mademoiselle Jeanne Vielliard, the Directress, Madame André Vernet, and Mademoiselle Elisabeth Pellegrin graciously gave me most useful comments and suggestions.

Furthermore, I am indebted to Mr. Gerard L. Carroll, a trustee of The Michael P. Grace, II, Trust, Mrs. Dorothy Deflandre, Executive Officer, U. S. Educational Foundation in Belgium, Mrs. Asta Ingeborg Ball *de Görlitz*, Mr. Peter Ford, my former student and now a Fulbright scholar in Paris, Dr. Francis Lazenby, Librarian at the Mediaeval Institute, Madame Lydie Murphy *de Mézières*, Miss Ingalill Gyllensten, Swedish Institute, Paris, and Miss Karin Eldblom in the Swedish National Travel Office, New York City. It is very pleasant for me to recall the many kindnesses shown me by Mr. Harold S. O'Brien, Resident Manager of the Savoy Hilton Hotel, New York City, who facilitated my stay in New York and my research in New York libraries.

Last but not least, heartfelt thanks are due to Mr. and Mrs. Wallace V. Bedolfe of Toronto, Canada, who so generously helped me to find the soul of Skara House in the distant Archives of Sweden and France, *quos Deus bene remuneret*.

PART I

HISTORY OF SKARA HOUSE

I

COLLEGES FOR SWEDISH AND
DANISH STUDENTS

Among the founders of colleges and hospices for the benefit of foreign students grouped into the English-German Nation at the mediaeval University of Paris, churchmen from Northern European areas, from Sweden and Denmark, showed great interest in providing their fellow countrymen with suitable accommodations. During the first four centuries of the University of Paris, from the earliest period until 1500, the following foundations were made for the members of the English-German Nation, one of the four Nations that constituted the Faculty of Arts in Paris : College of Dacia; College of Upsala; Skara House; College of Linköping or Linköping House; College of Scottish students; and House of the Germans. (Plate I).

Of these foundations, it is Skara House to which I particularly desire to call attention, because the rich archive material [1]) published for the first time in the third part of this book, the Chartulary, gives valuable information that was unknown to the few historians who have briefly mentioned Skara House.

Skara House is usually referred to as the College of Skara by modern historians of the University of Paris, although the records rarely speak of the property as a College but rather call it a

---

1) Paris, Archives Nationales, *M 73. Liasse B.* « Nation d'Allemagne. Titres des maisons de Notre Dame et du Cadran rue St. Jean de Beauvais. Sont joints les Statuts d'Association de la maison de l'Eglise de Scaren à l'enseigne N. D. au Clos Bruneau — autrement rue St. Jean de Beauvais, et deux quittances aux années 1483 et 1502 pour cens payés au chapitre de St. Benoit par la nation d'Allemagne à cause de la dite maison appellée l'hotel de Suecz ou Suède autrement de l'Image N. D. »

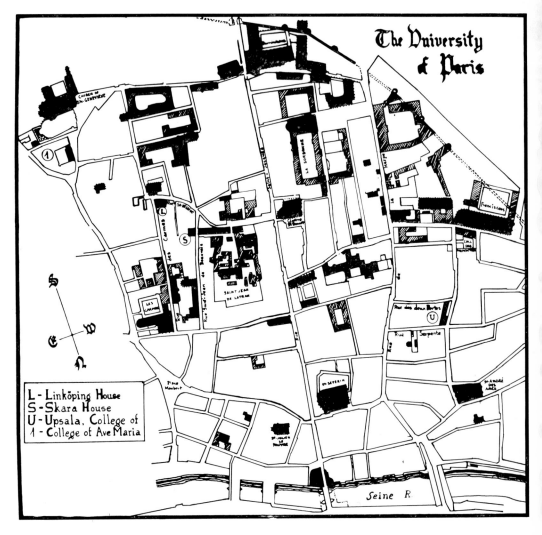

The University of Paris

L - Linköping House
S - Skara House
U - Upsala, College of
⋀ - College of Ave Maria

PLATE I

Location of the Houses for Swedish students
on the Left Bank in Paris.

Basic map in
F. Hoffbauer, *Paris à travers les âges,*
Paris, 1885, II. pl. VI.

house *(domus)*. I shall use the term Skara House; by it I mean the community of Swedish scholars living on the premises of the property of the canons of Skara.

The Skara House in Paris received its name from the Swedish city of Skara, because the Cathedral Chapter of this city had jurisdiction over the distant Paris property. Skara (Plate II) [2], one of the oldest towns in Sweden and the capital of Västergötland, with a present population of 8,832 (census of January 1, 1959), lies in the southern part of the country, in the old province of Skaraborg, near Lake Vänern, the largest lake in Sweden. To locate it on the map (13° 30' longitude and 58° 30' latitude), Skara is approximately 120 km. northeast of Göteborg and approximately 220 km. southwest of Stockholm. It is not very far from Husaby, where Sweden's Olaf Skötkonung was baptized at the well of Saint Sigfrid [3]. Skara's greatest monument today is its Cathedral, which, despite its recent restoration (Plate III), has retained its mediaeval charm and architectural splendor [4].

Because of the various nationalities of the officers of the English-German Nation, it was no longer clear to the proctors and receptors from areas far away from the Northern regions, centuries after the foundation of the Northern colleges, which houses or colleges were the property of the Nation and which belonged to certain provinces. Hence great confusion arose when those officers referred to these houses or colleges.

---

2) E. J. DAHLBERG, *Suecia antiqua et hodierna*, Stockholm, 1667-1716, a collection of 353 plates, views of cities and towns.

3) H. SWENSSON, *Skara i bild av Birgitta Flink*, Stockholm, 1952; G. MICHANEK, ed., *Skalder i Skara en antologi... med illustrationer av Stig Trägårdh*, Stockholm, [1952]; CH. RYDELL, *Skara, Urbs Gothorum vetustissima*, Upsala, 1719; L. MUSSET, *Les peuples scandinaves au moyen âge*, Paris, 1951, p. 131.

4) H. HILDEBRAND, *Skara domkyrka. Minnesskrift till den restaurerade domkyrkans invigning den 26 oktober 1894*, Stockholm, 1894, pp. 1-48.

If anyone today would like to assess the enthusiasm of mediaeval scholars and the number of difficulties surmounted by those journeying from the diocese of Skara to Paris, he should try making the trip today, in 1959, from Paris to Skara; assuming that he were to make use of the fastest railroad connections available, he would leave Paris on the Paris-Scandinavian express at 14.09 P. M., travel all night in order to get to København (Denmark) at 11 A. M., then board a train to the ferry-boat to Malmö, transfer at Malmö to another train in the direction of Göteborg, and there change to a small, slow, local train. If everything goes well, he will be in Skara late that night. If he is lucky, he will be there in time to enjoy the enchanting contour of the mediaeval Cathedral against the glow of boreal light.

In order to understand better the history of Skara House, we must know that three other houses or colleges had been founded in Paris for the benefit of foreign students from Sweden and Denmark : the *Domus Dacie*, the College of Upsala, and the College of Linköping or Linköping House.

The College of Dacia, bought as a hospice or hostel in 1275 by a « docteur du pays de Dace » [5]), changed its location several times. After 1430 it was located in Rue Gallande in the house called *Pomi Rubei*, near the Petit-Pont [6]), whither it had been moved from Rue de-la-Montagne-Sainte-Geneviève [7]). As it was not a Swedish property, I shall forego its history. I give in the next sections of this study only a brief summary of the histories of the College of Upsala and of Linköping House.

The dates of the foundations of these Colleges are known. The eminent Swedish historian Schück has given us valuable information on their history. But when he came to the history of Skara House he frankly admitted that he did not know of any printed or manuscript material concerning its origin and early history [8]).

As mentioned above, the various stipulations concerning ownership, rents, and cens to be paid to the colleges had sometimes been entirely forgotten several hundred years after the foundation of these colleges. Whenever dubious cases arose or apparently unlawful contestants appeared, the Nation would instruct its officers to verify the claims by consulting the title deeds referring to these houses. The more numerous the claims placed against a house, the

---

5) H. DENIFLE - AE. CHATELAIN, ed., *Chartularium Universitatis Parisiensis*, Parisiis, 1889, I, p. 536, n° 464 [henceforth referred to as *Chart. Univ. Paris*]; A. BUDINSZKY, *Die Universität Paris und die Fremden an derselben*, Berlin, 1876, p. 61.

6) BULAEUS [DU BOULAY], C. E., *Historia Universitatis Parisiensis*, Paris, 1665-73, V, p. 391 [henceforth referred to as DU BOULAY, *Hist. Univ.*]; A. BERTY - L. M. TISSERAND - C. PLATON, *Topographie historique du vieux Paris* [VI.] *Région centrale de l'Université*, Paris, 1897, p. 159; H. DENIFLE - AE. CHATELAIN, ed., *Liber procuratorum Nationis Anglicanae (Alemanniae) in Universitate Parisiensi*, Parisiis, 1937 [editio nova] II, 445, 534 [henceforth referred to as *Auct.* II].

7) « Collegio magistrorum et scholarium clericorum regni Dacie », *Chart. Univ. Paris.* III, p. 317, n° 1481; M. FÉLIBIEN - G. LOBINEAU, *Histoire de la ville de Paris*, Paris, 1725, v. 2, pt. 1 [IV], p. 224a.

8) H. SCHÜCK, « Svenska Pariserstudier under medeltiden », *Kyrkohistorisk Årsskrift* 1 (1900), p. 70. All that K. Kumlien says about the origin of the Skara House is that « it was probably bought during the time of Bishop Brynulphus Algotsson, that is, before 1317 » : K. KUMLIEN, « Svenskarna vid utländska universitet under medeltiden », *Historiska Studier tillägnade Sven Tunberg*, Uppsala, 1942, p. 152.

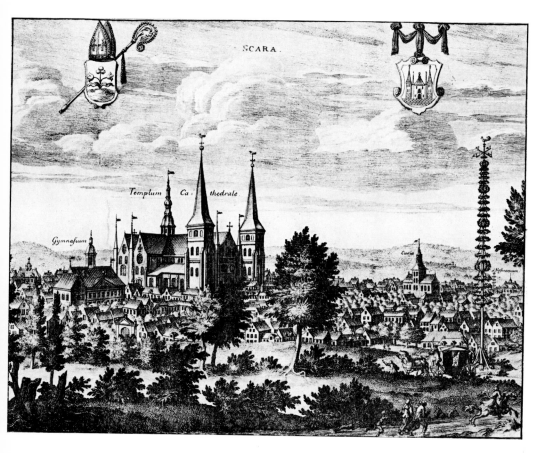

PLATE II

Skara.

After a copper engraving in
E. J. Dahlberg, *Suecia antiqua et hodierna,*
Holmiae [1667-1716], III, nº 41.

better and more careful was the search for the title deeds of the real estate properties.

Skara House was one of the most disputed colleges; the Nation was summoned many times before various authorities concerning the ownership of its properties. Hence the Nation's officials needed the earliest deeds of this House and consulted them many times [9]. Because of the frequent judicial contests, litigations, and legal proceedings in which Skara House was involved, the title deeds concerning the purchase of the House were carefully collected and kept together. They are preserved today at Paris, in the Archives Nationales, M 73, Liasse B [10].

---

9) In 1486 the Nation ordered its officers to consult the old title deeds of the House of Skara : C. SAMARAN - AE. A. VAN MOÉ, ed., *Liber procuratorum Nationis Anglicanae (Alemanniae)*, Parisiis, 1935, p. 595, 45 [henceforth referred to as *Auct.* III] : « dicta natio et procurator ejusdem nationis erant scitati ad compariendum [*sic*] in Castelleto pro quibusdam redditibus de domo Scarensi... Natio super [hoc] deliberavit quod viderentur *carte cum regestris.* »

10) The collection, consisting of 17 deeds, is analyzed in an inventory dated 1721, which is now in the Archives of the University of Paris, Sorbonne : Carton 14, 3e liasse, no 36, p. 4 : « Liasse B. [Domus Scarensis, Hotel de Suesse]. Titres des maisons de *Notre Dame* et du *Cadran* rue St. Jean de Beauvais [in clauso Brunello] ; cf. E. CHATELAIN, « Inventaire des Archives de la Nation d'Allemagne en 1721 », *Revue des bibliothèques* 1 (1891) 68-69. « Il y a dans cette liasse dix-sept chartes ou titres en date depuis l'an 1282 jusqu'à l'an 1502 » : Sorbonne, Carton 14, 3e liasse, no 36, *ibid.*

PLATE III

Cathedral of Skara.

Contemporary view.

II

THE COLLEGE OF UPSALA

Long before the foundation of the College of Upsala in a house located on Rue Serpente, Jacobus, archbishop of Upsala (1278-1281), set aside certain tythes, *decimas pauperum,* as early as 1280, to provide for students without sufficient means who were studying at Paris [1]. (Plate IV)

The property, consisting of a house, a garden, and a grange, where the College was established, was bought by Master Andreas And, provost of the Chapter of Upsala, in August 1285, from a certain William Pelterer *(pelliparius)* and Mathilda, his wife.

It was located in the censive of the King, on Rue Serpente, reaching southward to the Rue des Deux Portes *(ad vicum ad duas portes)* [2], between the house *Ad ensem* and that of Constancia, daughter of Thierricus [3]. In 1287, the house was listed under the name of a new owner, *Andree prepositi de Suessia* [4]. In 1291,

---

1) J. G. Liljegren, *Svenskt Diplomatarium. Diplomatarium Suecanum,* Stockholm-Holmiae, 1829, vol. I, p. 570, n° 699 [henceforth referred to as *D. S.*]; H. Schück, « Svenska Pariserstudier under medeltiden », *Kyrkohistorisk Årsskrift* 1 (1900) p. 44, n. 3; *Chart. Univ. Paris.,* I, p. 581, n° 496.

2) *D. S.* I, p. 663, n° 808; E. M. Olde, *De Universitate Parisiensi a Svecis Medio Aevo frequentata. Dissertatio* [Praes. J. H. Schröder] Upsaliae, 1830, p. 3, note 6; *Chart. Univ. Paris.* I, p. 581, n° 496, note.

3) The *D. S.* reads Thierrici Thendonis. In 1292 a certain Tierri l'Alemant [Teutonis ?] is mentioned in a *taille* as living in the neighborhood : H. Géraud, *Paris sous Philippe-le-Bel d'après des documents originaux et notamment d'après un manuscrit contenant le rôle de la taille imposée sur les habitants de Paris en 1292,* Paris, 1837, p. 157.

4) Taxed at 14 libr., *Chart. Univ. Paris.* II, p. 30, n° 556. Concerning Andreas (Anders) And, see : J. Peringskiöld, *Monumenta Ullerakerensia cum Upsalia nova illvstrata,* Stockholm, 1719, p. 190.

Upsala.

After a copper engraving in E. J. Dahlberg, *Suecia antiqua et hodierna*,
Holmiae [1667-1716], I, n° 56.

PLATE IV

Andreas gave it to the scholars of the diocese of Upsala, *scolaribus de nostra Upsalensi diocesi*. In a beautifully worded deed, Johannes Adolfi, archbishop of Upsala, promulgated the Statutes of the College, for a procurator and 12 students who would be under the supreme jurisdiction of the rector of the Cathedral School at Upsala [5]). (Plate V)

« Since the University of Paris, in which grains of knowledge are collected as a field of fertility bringing forth rich fruits, produces men abundant in a variety of virtues whose gracious abundance is copiously imparted to others, enlarging the small, teaching the unlearned, instructing the ignorant, and producing many virtuous men; the venerable master Andrew, provost of our Cathedral, diligently considering these things and observant of divine piety and ecclesiastical welfare, has granted to the students from our diocese of Upsala desiring to exert themselves in the aforesaid university for acquiring the good of learning and knowledge, from among the goods bestowed on him by God, a certain house of his in Paris on Rue Serpente, to be owned perpetually. »

Everyone who became a member of the House had to swear an oath in the presence of the proctor or proctors and the whole Community of scholars that he would observe the Statutes faithfully and not transgress them by contempt or deliberate malice.

The new fellow had to promise obedience to the rector of the Cathedral School at Upsala, who was, so to speak, the governor of the College of Upsala in Paris, and also to the proctor or proctors, his immediate superiors in Paris. Every newly-admitted fellow bound himself to leave the House and the Community of Swedish scholars immediately when requested to do so and not to use force in seeking readmission. He took an oath that in whatever status he

---

5) Edited in *D. S.* II, pp. 119-123, n° 1045; cf. OLDE, *De Univ. Paris a Svecis Medio Aevo frequentata*, pp. 4-10. Translation of the *Statutes* was done in my seminar on *Student Migrations* by Mr. JOHN SAUNDERS.

might be, he would accept the jurisdiction of the rector of the College in all matters pertaining to the College. The new fellow also had to agree that he would not refuse the office of proctor if appointed.

All who entered the College had to pledge that they would recite, either privately or with another fellow, the Hours of the Blessed Virgin on ferial days. Their recital was obligatory for the entire Community on feast days. Prayers preceded and followed the taking of meals. On feast days there was reading in the dining hall. On Sundays, on the vigils of saints, and on other festivities, the *Salve Regina* was chanted together.

Following the rules which prevailed at the College of Sorbonne [6]), the Statutes of the College of Upsala prohibited the fellow from eating privately in his room unless he was sick or too poor to pay the common expenses. In the latter case, with the permission of the superior of the House, the fellow could eat apart from the others. Students were not permitted to invite anybody to their rooms for food or drink, nor could they bring outsiders into the House without the permission of the proctor. Whoever violated these rules was fined, up to four *denarii*.

In the House everyone had to speak Latin except when speaking with servants or outsiders. Transgressors of this rule, after being warned three times, payed an *obolus* to the Community for each such offense.

The provosts were not required to give the Community an exact accounting of the operating expenses but only a general report.

In order that the scholarly atmosphere of the House be respected, nobody was allowed to speak too loud or cause noise or even sing in the house or in the garden on ferial days.

Chess, dice, and all other such games were strictly forbidden. No one could have dogs or falcons, apparently because hunting belonged only to the rich [7]). Violators of these rules were fined one *denarius;* if they persisted, the amount of the fine was left to the discretion of the proctor.

That fraternal charity might reign, no one was allowed to speak

---

6) A. L. Gabriel, « Robert de Sorbonne », *Revue de l'Université d'Ottawa* 23 (1953), 484-486; P. Glorieux, *Les origines du Collège de Sorbonne* (Texts and Studies in the History of Mediaeval Education, n° 8), Notre Dame, 1959, pp. 19-20.

7) P. E. Beichner, « Daun Piers, Monk and Business Administrator », *Speculum* 34 (1959), 611-619.

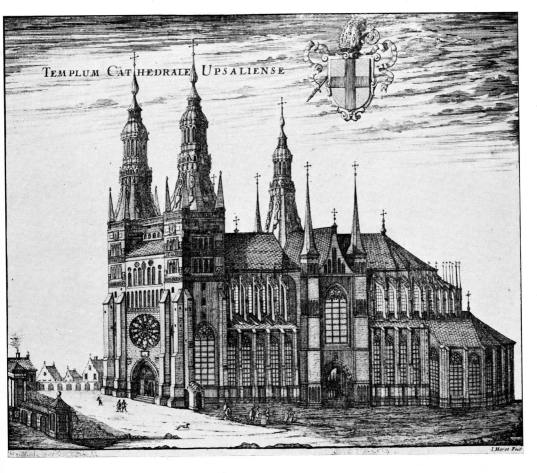

TEMPLUM CATHEDRALE UPSALIENSE

PLATE V

Seventeenth-century view of the Cathedral of Upsala.
French architect Etienne Bonneuill, « tailleur de pierre »,
worked on it after 1287.

After a copper engraving in
E. J. Dahlberg, *Suecia antiqua et hodierna*,
Holmiae [1667-1716], I, nº 57.

opprobrious or contentious words to his fellow students either in the College or outside of it. Whoever did the contrary had to pay two *solidi* to the Community and apologize or make restitution to the offended fellow. Incorrigible transgressors were expelled from the Community. If anyone raised his hand in violence against another student, he was expelled immediately, but could be readmitted after being absolved by the proctor and paying three Paris *solidi* to the Community. If any fellow damaged the house, he was obligated to make restitution, the nature of which depended upon the rector or the principal, and to pay ten Paris *solidi* to the Community for each offense. No one could remain outside after the curfew without reasonable cause or special permission from the principal. Transgressors were fined up to one Paris *denarius*. Students were forbidden to contract debts greater than four Paris *solidi* without the express permission of the proctor.

Solicitous attention was paid to the sick. If anyone became ill, a fellow was appointed by the principal to take care of him. When one was in his last agony and approaching death, all of the other business of the Community was postponed, and the dying person was piously commended to the Lord. Vigil was kept and the Psalter was faithfully recited over the body of the deceased person until the time of burial.

The principal had to promise under oath that he would exert diligent care and solicitude for the affairs of the Community. He was expected to report to the proctor all insubordinations and acts or words of insolence. The proctor, in turn, was obliged to hold a meeting with the Community four times a year, or more frequently if he deemed it necessary. In the meeting *(capitulum)* the fellows were reminded that no one should accuse another for the sake of vengeance but only for the sake of correction. Violators were fined an *obolus* for each offence.

The number of fellows was restricted to twelve. They were reminded that when their financial status would improve by the receiving of good benefices, they were to repay a fifteenth part of their benefices to the Community for as many years as they had enjoyed aid in Upsala College, providing that this aid consisted of twelve *denarii* weekly allowance besides lodging, wood, food, and bed linens. Those fellows who had received only the twelve *denarii* weekly allowance were bound to pay back a thirtieth part of their benefice. Those students whose aid consisted only of room, food, bed, and wood were to contribute to the support of the Paris

College according to their own discretion when their financial condition had improved.

The Statutes were read each week in the presence of all the fellows so that no one could excuse himself through ignorance or forgetfulness.

★

In 1299, Hemingus, canon of Upsala, left a certain amount of money in his will for the construction of a small building, *minoris domus,* to be attached to the existing College of Upsala [8]). The new house was built some time after the date of this grant. Its entrance was from Rue des Deux Portes.

On April 5, 1313, Andreas And transferred all of his rights concerning these houses [9]) to Nicholas, archbishop of Upsala (1308-1314). On July 30, 1315, he confirmed his decision, again assigning the rights to his property to the students from the diocese of Upsala, *domos inhabitandi, locandi et ordinandi* [10]). He specified the sites of the houses by stating that one, apparently the old one, faced Rue Serpente, the other, the new one, Rue des Deux Portes.

The new house, originally intended to be smaller, actually was larger than the old one; in 1329 only five students, Johannes de Suecia and four fellows, were living in the part facing Rue Serpente, but the other house, at the corner of Rue des Deux Portes and Rue de la Vieille Plâtrière, sheltered ten students [11]).

The house of Andreas And thus became the undisputed property of the diocese of Upsala. The Cathedral Chapter, even in its years

---

8) *D. S.* II, p. 287, n⁰ 1271 : « ... in edificacionem minoris domus vpsalensis existentis parisiis ».

9) *D. S.* III, pp. 122-123, n⁰ 1913 : « in uico serpentis, vna cum granchia uicina situata in uico inter duas portas ». The location of these two houses is confirmed by two documents dated respectively 1315 and 1354; *D. S.* III, p. 222, n⁰ 2025 : « domos sitas in vico serpentis Parisiis ex una parte, ex alia parte vero habentes vicum ad duas portas »; A. GEFFROY, « Les étudiants suédois à Paris, au quatorzième siècle », *Revue des Sociétés savantes* 5 (1858), p. 664, pièce n⁰ 1.

10) Text in *D. S.* III, 222, n⁰ 2025, and in Geoffroy, « Les étudiants suédois à Paris », pp. 663, 667-668, pièce n⁰ 4.

11) *Chart. Univ. Paris.* II, p. 663, n⁰ 1184. On *vicus Antiqui Plasterii* see JAILLOT, *Recherches critiques, historiques et topographiques sur la ville de Paris, depuis ses commencements connus jusqu'à présent*, Paris, 1782, V (Quartier Saint-André-des-Arcs), p. 40.

of poverty during 1321 and 1322, tried to find the necessary means
to support its students [12]). A section of the Upsala College was in
bad condition by the year 1341 *(quod periculum est in domo dictorum scolarium [de suessia]) * [13]). Henricus Ludwigsson, canon of
Upsala, in his will, dated May 8, 1346, gave five *marchae* for the
repair of the house [14]). In 1347 the house was still referred to as
in bad condition (Vielz places vides), belonging to the « escolliers
de Suesse » [15]).

The modest donation of Canon Ludwigsson was not sufficient to
save the building. In 1350 full authorization was given to Peter
Arnulfsson, canon of Upsala, and to Ingeldus Jonsson, clerk, to
sell the diocese of Upsala's tenements in Paris, since, according
to the statement of the jurors of the city of Paris (April 2, 1354),
the houses were « inustilles et non profitables aux diz escolliers »;
they were deserted and in a dilapidated condition *(platee vacue
inutiles)* [16]).

Apparently the proctors did not sell the entire property, for some
land or a garden *(platea seu ghardino)* remained in the possession
of the Upsala students [17]). On July 9, 1355, Ringvidus, archdeacon
of Upsala, and Master Ingimarus were appointed by the Archbishop and the Chapter of Upsala to act as their proctors and to
sell the remaining properties in Paris. They were instructed, however, to obtain first the consent of the rector and of the students
from Upsala, studying at Paris [18]).

The proctors' mission to Paris was not very successful, and they
returned home after appointing Petrus de Luca from Lombardy as
proctor of the Upsala property. A *littera procuracionis* was given
to him.

Petrus de Luca rented the Swedish property for 30 sol. paris. to

---

12) *D. S.* III, p. 536, no 2322; L. M. Bååth, *Diplomatarium Svecanum. Appendix.
Acta Pontificum Svecica I Acta Cameralia*, Holmiae, 1936-1942, I, p. 188, no 191.

13) *D. S.* V, pp. 82-83, no 3610.

14) *Ibid.*, p. 572, no 4074 : « Item pro edificio domorum Parisius quinque marchas ».

15) Berty, *Topographie historique*. [VI.] *Région centrale*, p. 565.

16) Geffroy, « Les étudiants suédois à Paris », 668, pièce no 5; 665.

17) H. Denifle - Ae. Chatelain, *Liber procuratorum Nationis Anglicanae (Alemanniae) in Universitate Parisiensi*, Parisiis, 1937 [editio nova] I, 429, 20 [henceforth
referred to as *Auct.* I].

18) *D. S.* VI, p. 563-564, no 5131. Original is in Stockholm, Riksarkivet no 229.
Ringvidus [Nicolai] died in 1360 : J. Peringskiöld, *Monumenta Ullerakerensia cum
Upsalia nova illvstrata*, Stockholm, 1719, pp. 207-208.

a certain master from Brittany who lived next to it. Meanwhile, around 1373, Thomas Graffardi [19]), secretary to the King of France, wanted to rent the property for 35 sol. paris. Petrus de Luca, however, refused to rent it, under the pretext that he was no longer the proctor of the tenement, because Ringvidus, who had given him the *littera procuracionis,* had died. But Thomas Graffardi, eager to obtain the property adjoining his own home, summoned Petrus Lucas to the Châtelet and tried to annoy him by suing for the repair of a wall that separated Thomas' house from the grounds of the Swedish college. Petrus inflexibly maintained that he was no longer proctor and consequently had nothing to do with the sale or upkeep of the estate.

Due to the fact that the property belonged to foreign students, the English-German Nation also became involved in the affair; it, too, was summoned to the Châtelet [20]). Since Thomas persisted in his efforts to acquire the house and land, the Nation saw it could acquire a new source of revenue by renting this abandoned property. Thomas even went so far as to promise the Swedish students that he would find them a new lot if they would abandon their claim to the dwellings on Rue Serpente until a later time. But the actual tenant, unwilling to give up the grounds, was deaf to the requests of the Nation and of the Swedish students mobilized by the Nation, that he allow Thomas the use of the property [21]).

On February 17, 1374, the English-German Nation summoned every Swedish student staying in Paris to its meeting in order to work out a contract between the Swedish students and the Nation on one hand and Thomas Graffardi on the other. Seeing the great eagerness of Thomas to obtain the garden, the Nation raised the rent to 40 sol. paris. [22]) and also made it clear that the province of Upsala had every right to the property [23]).

In 1392 Nicolaus de Bosco, bishop of Bayeux (1375-1408) [24]), sought possession of the garden of the Swedish college. We have

---

19) *Chart. Univ. Paris.* III, p. 265, n⁰ 1432. Studied medicine at the University of Paris; Master regent 1385-1394 : E. WICKERSHEIMER, *Dictionnaire biographique des médecins en France au moyen âge,* Paris, 1936, pp. 760-761.

20) *Auct.* I, p. 429, 16-45.

21) *Ibid.,* 438, 48 — 440, 39.

22) *Ibid.,* 443, 36 — 444, 11.

23) Thomas Graffardi paid *unum album* to the Nation in November 1376 and another in November 1377 : *Auct.* I, 509, 29; 528, 35.

24) C. EUBEL, *Hierarchia Catholica Medii Aevi* (ed. alt.) Monasterii, 1913, I, 125.

RUE SERPENTE
ET RUE DES DEUX PORTES
(B? ST GERMAIN)
ETAIT
LE COLLEGE DE SUESSE
OU D'UPSAL
FONDE EN 1291
POUR LES ETUDIANTS SUEDOIS
DE L'UNIVERSITE DE PARIS
1934

PLATE VI

A plaque mounted on the corner of
15 Rue Serpente and Rue Hautefeuille, Paris,
marking the site of the mediaeval College of Upsala.

no records that establish how and when he obtained it. However, because of a decision by the University of Paris and its rector *(ex deliberatione Universitatis et sentencia rectoris)* that other foreign possessions such as the Colleges of Dacia and of Linköping and Skara House be placed under the jurisdiction of the Nation in 1392, the Nation also claimed the same rights over the Upsala property [25]. In April, 1392, the bishop of Bayeux offered 32 francs to the Nation for the property, with the provision that should the Swedish students at any future date claim the land and dwellings as their own, the Nation would have to recompensate them. On November 9, 1393, the University gave the English-German Nation permission to conclude an agreement with the bishop concerning the Swedish property in Rue Serpente [26]. Since, in the inventory of the properties of the Nation *(Inventarium bonorum nationis)* drawn up in 1442, this possession of Upsala is not referred to, although the other Swedish houses belonging to the dioceses of Linköping and Skara are explicitly mentioned [27]), we infer that the bishop of Bayeux did acquire the property.

The memory of the College of Upsala is commemorated today by a plaque that can be seen at the corner of the intersection formed by 15 Rue Serpente and Rue Hautefeuille (Plate VI). It is mounted 25 to 30 feet above the ground, on the *premier étage*. The size of this plaque is, I would say, about 3 feet square. The inscription reads :

RUE SERPENTE

ET RUE DES DEUX PORTES

(B^D ST. GERMAIN)

ETAIT

LE COLLEGE DE SUESSE

OU D'UPSAL

FONDE EN 1291

POUR LES ETUDIANTS SUEDOIS

DE L'UNIVERSITE DE PARIS

1934

25) *Auct.* I, 661, 27.
26) *Ibid.*, 670, 27-35; 674, 8-20; 681, 15; 684, 40.
27) *Auct.* II, 534, 3-31.

III

THE COLLEGE OF

LINKÖPING

Another Swedish property in Paris was the College of Linköping, or rather Linköping House, which also belonged to a Cathedral Chapter, that of Linköping. The House was purchased in 1317 by the archdeacon Johannes, Philippus, Haraldus, and Erlandus, all canons from Linköping, for 24 libr. paris., paid to Everardus de Campis, canon and chamberlain of the Church of Saint-Marcel at Paris [1]).

The house was commonly referred to as « At the Sign of the Stag's Antlers » *(Ad Cornu Cervi)*. It was located on Rue Saint-Hilaire, probably at the corner of this street and the western side of Rue des Carmes, facing the College of Lombards *(ante Collegium Lumbardorum)*. More precisely, it was between Rue des Carmes, Rue Saint-Hilaire, and a narrow passage called Rue Josselin, east of Skara House [2]). This confirms Berty's finding about a house « Maison de la Corne de Cerf » described in a deed of 1240 as « Maison où il y a ung four, au carrefour Sainct Hilaire, faisant le coing de la rue Sainct Hilaire, chargée envers le chapitre de Saincte Agnès » [3]).

---

1) E. M. Olde, *De Univ. Paris a Svecis Medio Aevo frequentata*, Litt. A., p. ii, cf. H. Schück, *Ecclesia Lincopensis. Studier om Linköpingskyrkan under medeltiden och Gustav Vasa* (Acta Universitatis Stockholmiensis n⁰ 4), Stockholm, 1959, pp. 43-47; 595.

2) *Auct.* II, 534, 24; « de vico Josselini retro ante dictam domum *ad cornu cervi* », *ibid.*, 830, 32. On rue Josselin see my chapter on *Topography*, note 10; cf. *D. S. n. s.* II, p. 847, n⁰ 2000.

3) Berty, *Topographie historique* [VI.] *Région centrale*, p. 339.

The house was in the censive of Saint-Marcel, and formerly belonged to Guillelmus Doll. At times the student body living there between 1329-1336 was smaller than in the College of Upsala or Skara House : only three students were registered during this time by the University *taxatores* [4]).

In May 1375, we find the above property deserted by the students belonging to Linköping diocese; apparently, however, it was used by other scholars from the Kingdom of Sweden. Confusion arose in regard to the legitimate proctorship of the House. Winandus, provost of the Cathedral of Åbo, maintained against Master Johannes de Gortenbeke, *doctor decretorum*, in May 1375, that he had been appointed by Nicolaus Hermanni (Nils Hermansson), bishop of Linköping (1375-1391), to act as the rightful proctor of the House. Johannes de Gortenbeke, on the other hand, claimed that he had been designated as *substitutus procurator* by the previous procurator, who in turn had been appointed by Gotscaldus Falcdol (1364-1374) [5]), predecessor of the present bishop. To settle the dispute, no lesser man was delegated to see Winandus than the famous philosopher Marsilius de Inghen, who later, in 1386, became the first rector of the University of Heidelberg [6]).

By April 1392, the House was wholly abandoned by Swedish students, and, together with Skara House, it was entrusted to the care of the English-German Nation. From that time, the fate of the Linköping House was more or less similar to that of Skara House; both caused much worry and anxiety to the Nation. First, the House of Linköping needed repairs in 1393. By February 1394 some repairs had been made, but they were insufficient, since in July 1395 the sub-beadle reported severe damages : the roof had fallen down and the tenant wanted to move out. Additional repairs were made in about eight months. The whole cost of the reconstruction amounted to 415 francs, 10 sol., and 11 den. paris., as was announced by the receptor on June 7, 1396 [7]). In February 1396, the House was rented to Johannes Bonrode for 25 francs, in June 1396

---

4) *Chart. Univ. Paris.*, II, p. 662b, nº 1184.

5) *Auct.* I, 471, 34 — 472, 22.

6) G. RITTER, *Die Heidelberger Universität. Erster Band. Das Mittelalter (1386-1508)*, Heidelberg, 1936, p. 64, plate 2; E. GILSON, *History of Christian Philosophy in the Middle Ages*, New York, 1955, p. 519.

7) *Auct.* I, 661, 35; 678, 31; 688, 8; 706, 39; 707, 1; 708, 22; 709, 11, 34; 725, 1, note 1.

to a certain abbot, then to a Picard Master, Thomas Maerscalli, who moved out before February 1398 [8]).

The Nation was in critical financial condition when the House became vacant; rent revenue was greatly needed in order to renovate one of the Nation's schools, the *Scole Septem Artium Liberalium* [9]).

In May 1399, the House was leased again to a certain Lombard for 24 *scuta* and 1 franc; then, in July, to some masters from Scotland for 25 francs. The menacing plague forced the Scots to leave Paris in great haste and without notifying the Nation. Later, however, they announced that they did not intend to return. New tenants were found, in the person of Master Johannes Dorp in June 1400, and, later, in Johannes Picard [10]).

The House needed repairs again in 1403. On January 2, 1404, the Nation decided to sell all of the revenues *(redditus)* received from the House and to use the money for purposes of restoration. After much bickering as to the financially most advantageous procedure to be used in making the repairs, the House was on May 22, 1405, rented again to Master Johannes Dorp for 20 *scuta*, and later in 1405 to Master Guillelmus Blok, whose rate was raised in 1406 to 22 *scuta*. The Nation turned down the proposal of a certain Master Richardus [Ioenen ?], who was willing to lend 50 francs to the Nation for repairs of the House but asked that his rent be fixed at 5 francs yearly [11]).

Fortunately, at the beginning of 1407, several important scholars arrived at Paris from Sweden. There seems to have been a concerted effort by the Cathedral Chapters of Skara and Linköping to launch an offensive for the repossession of their properties from the English-German Nation. Siggo Uddsson, canon of Skara, was the spokesman of Skara Chapter; Nicolaus Skrilvara [Skrilmara, Skrifvare ?], dean, represented the interests of Linköping [12]). (Plate VII)

The Nation attempted the same delaying tactics for Linköping

---

8) *Ibid.*, I, 717, 36, 45; 725, 10; 761, 38.

9) On the school see G. C. BOYCE, *The English-German Nation in the University of Paris during the Middle Ages*, Bruges, 1927, 123-133; *Auct.* I, 770, 32; 772, 11; 789, 28.

10) *Auct.* I, 803, 31; 806, 44; 814, 23; 816, 12; 851, 32.

11) *Ibid.*, I, 860, 29; 873 - 875; 882, 5; 886, 23; 905, 22; 907, 27; 908, 20.

12) *Ibid.*, I, 916, 2; 920, 19.

as it had used for Skara. It requested the refund of all the moneys it had paid for the repair of the House during the absence of its proper owners. The dean accepted the conditions, but could not control his temper and *in suo furore* told the Nation what he thought of its maneuvering. This was a good opportunity for the Nation to show its « dignity ». Nicolaus was summoned before the Nation, and one of the masters « eloquently and severely » *(eloquenter et aspere)* reprimanded him, the representative of the lawful owners. On September 23, 1400, the dean was told to pay 40 *scuta* in gold and 60 *scuta* in securities. He would not, however, secure possession of the House until the total amount spent by the Nation on repairs had been repaid to the last cent *(de ultimo denario)* [13].

News of the acquisition of these unexpected revenues by the English-German Nation must have reached the ears of the Chapter of Saint-Marcel in Paris. Its canons reminded the Nation, on November 11, 1406, that it had neglected to pay the obligatory *census annualis* for the House which was located in its censive. The Nation was told to produce the deed of amortization or else the House would be turned over to the King [14].

On the next day, November 12, however, the dean of Linköping paid the Nation 35 *scuta* in gold and 25 in silver, and gave securities for the rest (40) : a copy of the *Decretum* and three golden rings with precious stones. In a solemn gathering on that date the Nation took the dean to the House and showed him the repairs that had been made. Pierre Cauchon, later archbishop of Beauvais and prominent in the trial of St. Joan of Arc, who enjoyed the confidence of both the Nation and the Swedes, was also present. Irksome as it was for the dean, he still could not get the House back. Before the Nation would give a receipt and detailed accounting of the repairs made on Linköping property, it demanded the balance of 26 *scuta*, 14 sol. and 8 den. [15]. And, even should full reimbursement be made, the Nation desired to have possession of the property until June 24, 1407, apparently to obtain rent for the full year.

---

13) *Ibid.*, I, 924, 20; 932, 9; 933, 22.

14) *Ibid.*, I, 934, 39; on Saint-Marcel cf. M. L. CONCASTY, « Le bourg Saint Marcel à Paris, des origines au XVIᵉ siècle », *Positions des thèses de l'Ecole des Chartes*, 1937, pp. 25-37.

15) *Auct.*, I, 936, 15.

Templum Chathedrale Lincopense.

FVNDATIO TEMELL.LIN:

ANO CHRI 813 FVNDATVM EST HOC TEMPLVM SVB REGE BERONE TERTIO. AÑO 1260.AD OCCIDETALE AVCTV
EST 40 VLNAS SVB REGE WOLDEMARO QVI HIC CORONAT, EST AÑO AÑO 1251.AÑO 1400.AD ORIENTALE.
ADAVCTVM TRIBVS CHORIS SVBREGE ERICO POMER: ET ABSOLVTVM ANO 1499 SVB REGE IOHANNE 2.
COMBVSTVM EST HOC TÊPIV QVATER: AÑO 1416 SVB REGE ERICO POMERANO.AÑO 1490 SVB GVBERNATORE
STENONE STVRE..ANO 1546 SVB REGE GVSTAVO PRIMO.AÑO 1567 SVB REGE ERICO 14.AÑO 1465. OBIIT
CATILL, EPs LINCOP.

PLATE VII   Seventeenth-century view of the Cathedral of Linköping.

After a copper engraving in E. J. Dahlberg, *Suecia antiqua et hodierna,*
Holmiae [1667-1716], III, n° 5.

On January 9, 1407, both parties agreed to entrust the resolution of their differences to arbiters. They elected men as socially and scholastically prominent as Pierre Cauchon and Oliverius de Imperio, book-dealer *(librarius)* of the University of Paris. The arbiters came to the following conclusions : 1) The dean should receive the accounts of the repairs made on Linköping House together with a receipt for the money he had paid to the Nation; — 2) the dean owes only 12 *scuta;* — 3) the dean could take possession of the House for himself and the students of the diocese of Linköping *(sue ecclesie scolaribus)* after June 24, 1407. An agreement was drawn up by Johannes Guberstat, notary public, and the solemn investiture for the ownership of the House took place in the Church of Sainte-Geneviève on March 13, 1407 [16]).

The acquisition of the House put a considerable financial burden upon the unprosperous Chapter of Linköping. Contributions requested for the Paris property [17]) were behind schedule, and far from being generous. Both Bishop Kanutus, in a letter dated June 30, 1407, and the Cathedral Chapter, in a summons issued on November 23 of the same year, energetically exhorted their subjects to support the Linköping House at Paris [18]).

In 1410 the Cathedral Chapter of Linköping appointed Siggo Uddsson, canon of Skara, as procurator of the House; but the *Liber procuratorum* of the Nation is silent about his activities and it is doubtful whether he accepted the office [19]). Soon another procurator was named in the person of Johannes Hildebrandi, who received on September 1, 1414, from Master Fredericus Trask, canon of Åbo, 12 *scuta* in French currency as a contribution from the Cathedral Chapter of Linköping in behalf of the house *Ad Cornu Cervi in vico Sancti Hylarii apud Car-*

---

16) *Ibid.*, I, 941, 45 — 942, 39; *Auct.* II, 8, 14. This agreement might be that « littera compromissi super reparacionibus factis in domo Lincopie tam pro parte nacionis, quam pro parte illorum de episcopatu » which was kept in the Nation's *archa* and listed in an inventory of 1424 : *ibid.*, II, 320, 21.

17) « ... domus ecclesie nostre Lincopensis Parisius pro clericis studentibus » : *D. S. n. s.* I, pp. 654-665, n⁰ 855; OLDE, *De Univ. Paris. a Svecis Medio Aevo frequentata*, p. iii.

18) « subsidio pauperum scolarium ac subsidio per euiccione domus Parisiensis » : *D. S. n. s.* I, p. 690, n⁰ 902; cf. 1408 [?], February 27 : « ... et subsidio pro euictione domus Parisiensis dudum indicto », *D. S. Appendix*, I/II, p. 206, n⁰ 994.

19) SCHÜCK, *op. cit.*, 68.

melitas [20]). Although the *Liber procuratorum* does not mention them, some students from Linköping must have been staying in Paris, probably studying in the higher faculties, for in August 1414 an otherwise not identified canon from Linköping sent from Paris a most enthusiastic letter to Kanutus, bishop of Linköping, about the University, whose glory, he writes, is much greater than one may believe, to judge merely by its reputation *(quia mayor est gloria eius quam rumor)* [21]).

It was probably the same canon who wrote to the Cathedral Chapter in Linköping, on September 5, 1414, encouraging them to send students to Paris. Perhaps the life is more expensive, he wrote, but at Paris even an *artista*, a young student at the Faculty of Arts, could learn much *(imo multum artiste proficere possunt)*. Thanks to this lover of Paris, we have some approximate figures dealing with the cost of living of University people. Those in higher faculties needed 50 crowns *(coronae)*, while a young artista could manage with only 16 *nobiles* a year [22]) at the University of Paris.

The next report from the House dates from September 16, 1430. The procurator of the House, a certain Georgius, *licentiatus in decretis*, was in jail and the House was left without custody. The Nation drew up an inventory and listed some items as belonging to the House and others to Boemundus, beadle of the Nation, and to the absent students *(aliquorum scolarium absentium)*. It was a prudent decision, because by October 6 a certain villein *(rusticus)* was living in the House, and someone from the Royal Palace *(in pallacio regis)* who claimed the rights to the proctorship, was ready to contribute something towards the repairs of the House. The Nation, fearing that it might lose the House to an outsider, appointed Boemundus as *comprocurator* to negotiate with the procurator concerning necessary repairs.

By October 22, 1436, the House was almost in ruins; the repairs would cost 200 *scuta,* but the Nation had no money *(nullam pecu-*

---

20) « in moneta regia et argentea pronunc currente in regno Francie » : *D. S. n. s.* II, p. 847, n⁰ 2000.

21) *Ibid.*, p. 841, n⁰ 1990. After 1410, the northern German universities, particularly Rostock and Greifswald, were favored by the students of Linköping, but clerks with richer prebends went to Leipzig, Erfurt, Vienna, Cologne, Louvain, and the Italian universities : H. Schück, *Ecclesia Lincopensis*, pp. 488-520; 610-611.

22) *Ibid.*, p. 848, n⁰ 2001.

niam habebat) [23]). The Nation, therefore, decided to demolish the House and store the material in the back yard until someone from Linköping came to claim it. The well-to-do beadle Boemundus was charged with the task. The members of the Nation received a gloomy report on the House on February 9, 1437 : The House *Ad Cornu Cervi* was without a roof, the beams were rotted, and construction-parts had been stolen. It seemed to the Nation that the only solution was to sell the building material of the House. The proposal was almost accepted when Laurencius Olavi de Thuna [24]) objected on July 7, 1437, thus preventing the disappearance of the building on Rue Saint-Hilaire. He even went further, and convinced the Nation that it should rebuild the House. Apparently, however, no action followed the resolution, because in 1442 the House was still in miserable condition [25]).

On September 30, 1449, the Nation again became alarmed, because a certain Master Johannes Penneser wanted to alienate the property on the grounds that he had carried out the repair of the wall between his house and that of Linköping. Penneser had been cunning : he had found a tenant for Linköping House who at his request willfully neglected the repair of the wall in order that Penneser could claim it at the Royal Court as abandoned property. The legal brains of the Nation found an easy and quick solution. They argued that Boemundus was the legitimate proctor, because he had been appointed procurator by the Swedes when they left Paris *(per magistros illius provincie in recessu eorum de Parisius)*; consequently Boemundus should protest and resist any attempt at alienation [26]).

---

23) *Auct.* II, 437, 45; 441, 40; 446, 6; 447, 33; 490, 27.

24) Laurencius Olavi de Thuna was a canon of Upsala; the University recommended to the archbishop of Upsala on September 18, 1436 or 1437 that Laurencius, though absent from Upsala, retain his benefice : *Auct.* II, Intr. xvi-xx. Bachelor of Prague, as he asserted, he was examined by the Nation and was received as such : *ibid.*, 491, 23. (There were two persons named Laurentius Olavi at the University of Prague around 1406-7, a Laurentius Olavi canon of Upsala, and a Laurentius Olavi archdeacon of Vesterås : *Monumenta Historica Universitatis Carolo-Ferdinandeae Pragensis*, Praguae, 1834, II, p. 156-157. I do not think that Laurencius Olavi de Thuna is to be identified with either). Lic. and mag. Art. in 1437 (*Auct.* II, 494, 33, 40). I do not know if he is the Laurencius Olavi de Upsala who registered at the University of Rostock in 1448 : A. HOFMEISTER, *Die Matrikel der Universität Rostock*, Rostock, 1889, I, 85; ANNERSTEDT, *Upsala Universitets Historia*, Upsala, 1877, I, 10.

25) *Auct.* II, 492, 17; 494, 1; 497, 25, 32; 534, 28.

26) *Ibid.*, II, 781, 40 — 782, 39.

This is the last report we know of concerning the House of Linköping. A few years later Boemundus died [27]), and the property must have slipped out of the hands of the Nation. Later inventories do not mention it. The only Swedish property that survived all adversities and was saved for the English-German Nation was Skara House.

---

27) November or December 1453, *Auct.* II, 901, n. 7.

IV

THE ORIGIN

OF SKARA HOUSE :

THE HOUSE IN CLOS-BRUNEAU

Skara House, called *Domus Scarensis, Hotel Suesce, Domus ad Imaginem Nostre Domine,* is mentioned for the first time on January 13, 1284, in a deed of Guillelmus, archdeacon and *Officialis* of the bishop of Paris. It mentioned a building consisting of two contiguous houses, looking almost as one unit, and of a grange [1]. The good description of the House given by the *Officialis* will help us later on to understand better the topography of the properties of the English-German Nation during the fifteenth century.

This house, which originally belonged to beadle Guillelmus Biterne (Betourne, Bisterne) and his wife Johanna, was situated in the *censive* of the Abbey of Sainte-Geneviève; the grange was in the *censive* of Saint-Benoît [2]. Beadle Biterne was still living when the deed was issued; a year later, on February 18, 1285, he was referred to as the « servant » of the French Nation [3], an expression which designated the beadle in the service of the French Nation of the Faculty of Arts in Paris.

---

1) Paris, Arch. Nat. M 73, n° 1 [I] : « super domo et grangia Guillelmi dicti Biterne sibi ad inuicem contiguis et qualibet eorum insolidum sitis. » The Roman numerals in brackets are mine and refer to the documents edited in Part III, the *Chartulary.*

2) It seems that one of the buildings had been previously owned by Guillebertus de Volta : M 73, n° 8 [VIII]; n° 10 [XI].

3) *Chart. Univ. Paris.,* I, p. 628, n° 519 : « communi servienti in natione Gallicorum. »

PLATE VIII

Växjö.

After a copper engraving in
E. J. Dahlberg, *Suecia antiqua et hodierna*,
Holmiae [1667-1716], III, n° 80.

The house of Biterne was charged with various cens and rents. A 1276 *censier* of the Abbey of Sainte-Geneviève informs us that Guillelmus Biterne owed 15 sol. to the Abbey [4]). On January 13, 1284, Richardus Tesson [5]), *clericus*, later canon of Notre-Dame, bought 6 sol. 9 den. paris. « revenues », which had been received on the house previously by Johannes de Volta, son of Guillebertus de Volta (Voute, Vouta) [6]). Canon Tesson must have had some further plans for the house, probably purchase, because on February 6, 1285, he bought another yearly revenue of 14 sol. paris., received on the house previously by Philippus Carpentarius and his wife Alipdis.

As the title deeds of Skara House, summarized in the Chartulary, reveal, Guillelmus Biterne and his wife Johanna had three daughters : Thomassia [7]), Isabellis [8]), and Johanna. Thomassia was married to Guillelmus de Orvalle (Orval), later the owner of the house; Isabellis, to Thomas de Tyha, *clericus;* and Johanna, to Jacobus Hure [9]).

After the death of Guillelmus Biterne (around 1286-87), Isabellis and Johanna renounced all their hereditary rights in favor of their sister Thomassia and her husband, Guillelmus de Orvalle. The latter lived in the house before Easter 1289; Guillelmus de Orvalle is mentioned that year by the taxing officers of the University of Paris as possessing a house in *Clauso Brunelli* [10]).

---

4) Paris, Arch. Nat. S. 1626^1 : *Recepta pitanciarum conventus Sancte Genovefe Paris. in Monte*, [1276] *a termino Sancti Remigii usque ad Natale*, fol. 5 verso : [in clauso Brunelli] « Guillelmus Biterne, .xv. den. et totidem in aliis terminis pro domo sua in qua manet sita iuxta domum Radulphi Scriptoris eodem vico. » Cf. also fol. 16 verso; fol. 23 verso; fol. 31 recto.

5) M 73, n° 1 [I]. In 1284 he was referred to as only a *clericus;* on February 26, 1285, as *canonicus* of Notre-Dame in Paris. He died around February 25, 1295 : M. GUÉRARD, *Cartulaire de l'Eglise Notre-Dame de Paris*, Paris, 1850, IV, 17; cf. *Ibid.*, III, 94; A. MOLINIER, *Obituaires de la province de Sens* T. I. (Diocèses de Sens et de Paris), Paris, 1902, pt. 1, p. 106.

6) A 1276 *censier* of Sainte-Geneviève mentions a vicus Nicholai de Vota [Volta] : A. GUESNON, « Un collège inconnu des Bons Enfants d'Arras à Paris du XIIIe au XVe siècle », *Mémoires de la Société Historique de Paris*, 42 (1915), 14.

7) M 73, n° 3 [III]; n° 5 [V].

8) M 73, n° 3 [III].

9) M 73, n° 4 [IV].

10) *Chart. Univ. Paris.*, II, p. 31, n° 556. The house was taxed at 6 lib. 10 sol. paris.

V

PURCHASES OF EMPHASTUS,
CANON OF VÄXJÖ

The property in Clos-Bruneau recently inherited by Guillelmus de Orvalle [1]) and Thomassia was bought on September 10, 1292, by a Swedish scholar in Paris, Emphastus (Anfaste, Hemfredus, Hemphastus), canon of Växjö, for 60 lib. paris. Emphastus at this time was serving in the Cathedral Chapter of Växjö under Bishop Magnus [2]), the successor of Boethius, who died in 1291.

The city of Växjö (Plate VIII), capital of Småland, is approximately 200 km. northeast of Lund, 340 km. southwest of Stockholm, and 200 km. southwest of Skara. Its present population is 23,578 (census of January 1, 1960). The Church of Växjö [3]) is mentioned for the first time by Eskil, archbishop of Lund, in a deed of 1170, to which Balduinus, bishop of Växjö, acted as witness [4]). The Church was burned down in 1277 by the Danes. Its reconstruction was left to Bishop Boethius and his successor Magnus.

The 1292 seal of the Chapter of Växjö recalls the memory of

---

1) The property that was to become Skara House is mentioned in 1289 by the *taxatores* of the University : « Domum Guillelmi de Orval, in clauso Burnelli; VI. libr. et X sol. de Paris, » *Chart. Univ. Paris.*, II, p. 31, n⁰ 556.

2) P. B. Gams, *Series episcoporum Ecclesiae Catholicae*, Leipzig, 1931, 341; Eubel, *Hierarchia Catholica*, I, 524-5.

3) H. Berg - I. Svalenius, *Växjö stads historia, tiden fram till 1718*, Växjö, 1956, p. 58.

4) Among the more noteworthy bishops of Växjö were Gregorius (1221, 1248); Asserus (1266); Boetius (1288, died 1291); Magnus (1295, 1320); Boetius (1320, died 1343). Eubel, I, 524-525; C. Annerstedt, *Scriptores rerum Suecicarum medii aevi*, Upsaliae, 1871-1876, III, 2, pp. 129-30.

PLATE IX

Seal of the Cathedral Chapter
of Växjö (1292).

Diplomatarium Suecanum
[henceforth referred to as *D. S.*] nº 1075.
Enlarged; orig. 60 mm.

Växjö's three martyrs : Unaman, Sunaman, and Vinaman [5]). According to the Vita of Saint Sigfrid, they came to Sweden with their uncle Saint Sigfrid at the invitation of King Olaf for missionary work around Växjö, where they built a church. The legend would have it that the three brothers were killed by pagans [6]), and that their heads were cut off, put in a pail, and thrown into a nearby lake. Saint Sigfrid, having heard the sad news, returned to Varend. Miraculously, three starlike lights shining above the lake revealed the position of the three heads [7]). Saint Sigfrid placed them in the Church of Växjö where they were subsequently venerated [8]).

The 1292 seal of the Cathedral Chapter of Växjö portrays the three blood-streaming heads emerging from the water, Unaman's in the center, with the two others facing it. The miraculous star is above the head of the left figure, while the miracle-producing Hand of God appears in the right upper field (Plate IX). The seal is round, 60 mm., with the legend : [† SIGIL] LVM. CAPITVLI. WEXIONENSIS [9]).

Emphastus' purchase was made almost a year after Andreas And, provost of Upsala, left his home to the students from the diocese of Upsala, for whom John, archbishop of Upsala, had promulgated Statutes between April 23 and 28, 1291 [10]).

It is likely that the efforts of Emphastus were encouraged by Brynulphus, bishop of Skara (1278, August 2 - 1317, February 6) who, according to testators at his canonization process, had spent many years in study at the University of Paris [11]).

---

5) *Analecta Bollandiana*, 60 (1942), 88, T. Schmid, « Trois légendes de saint Sigfrid » : « Erant autem in comitatu suo [Sigfridi], inter ceteros viros religiosos tres nepotes eius, videlicet Unamannus, sacerdos, Sunamannus dyaconus et Vynamannus subdyaconus ».

6) « Dyabolus autem, tocius boni invidus emulator, adversus nepotes sancti Sigfridi XII viros concitavit, qui nocte domum eorum intrantes trucidabant eos, precidentes capita eorum » : *ibid.*, p. 83. On the legend of Saint Sigfrid, cf. E. G. Geijer - J. H. Schröder, *Scriptores rerum Svecicarum*, Upsaliae, 1828, II, 347-367; *Analecta Bollandiana*, 45 (1927), 373; 52 (1934), 117-20; 57 (1939), 163-4; 59 (1941), 344; also BHL nn. 7706-7708.

7) « Vidit in stagni medio tria luminaria ad modum stellarum micancia » : *Analecta Bollandiana*, 60 (1942), 89.

8) H. Berg - I. Svalenius, *Växjö stads historia*, pp. 46-48.

9) *D. S.*, II, p. 144, no 1075 : deed of July 20, 1292.

10) *D. S.*, II, pp. 112-123, no 1045; Olde, *De Univ. Paris. a Svecis Medio Aevo frequentata*, pp. 4-10; cf. chapter II, note 5.

11) C. Annerstedt, ed., *Scriptores Rerum Svecicarum*, Upsaliae, 1871-1876, III, 2, ch. 66, p. 162 : « Ipse beatus Brynulphus primo erat in studio Parisiensi IX annis,

Brynulphus [Brynolf Algotsson] came from a well known family of Västergötland. After his studies at the University of Paris, he returned to Sweden and was elected bishop of Skara. A wise and holy pontiff, he enjoyed the friendship of the King except for a brief period from 1288 to 1290. Saint Louis' son Philippe III le Hardi, had given a fragment of the Holy Thorn to King Magnus Lagaböter. The latter's son, Håkan Magnusson, gave part of it to Brynulphus in 1304 [12]).

> Dies est laetitiae,
> dies gloriosa
> qua datur Westgotiae
> spina pretiosa...

The holy bishop's devotion to the Holy Thorn is recalled today in the Chapel erected in honor of Brynulphus in the newly restored Skara Cathedral.

> Supplicamus Jesu Bone
> nos perducas vi corone
> ad coronam glorie.
> Tua spina nos confortet
> ut mens nostra leta portet
> spinas penitentie [13]).

Brynulphus' oval-shaped seal (85 × 50 mm.), dating from 1281, bears the effigy of a mitered bishop seated on a throne adorned

---

et inde veniens in castrum Bagahws, Asloensis diocesis, dominus Rex... ad alios IX annos ipsum remisit ad studium Parisiense predictum. » Another witness said (ibid., ch. 9, p. 141) : « Item quod ipse sanctus Brynolphus... nunc orationibus devote intentus fuit, nunc frequenti vacauit studio quod Parisius XVIII annis, vel quasi, continuo compleuit. » Cf. ibid., ch. 27, p. 147.

12) H. SWENSSON, Skara i bild av Birgitta Flink, Stockholm, 1952, pp. 35, 37; Y. BRILIOTH, Svenska Kyrkans Historia. II. Den senare medeltiden 1274-1521, Stockholm - Uppsala, [1941], pp. 167-170.

13) According to a witness of his canonization process, « Rex Francie contulit Regi Swecie tunc temporis vnam spinam de corona spinea domini nostri saluatoris, Rex autem Swecie contulit eam dicto beato Brynolpho tunc episcopo Scarensi, qui ex eius veneratione et deuotione plurimum allectus, fecit nouam historiam de eadem corona spinea domini, referens se ad ecclesiam Scarensem, eo quod omni anno ibidem in venerationem dicte spinee corone domini eadem hystoria canitur secundum institutionem ipsius beati Brynolphi » : ANNERSTEDT, Scriptores rerum Svecicarum, III, 2, ch. 34, p. 150.

PLATE X

Seal of
Brynulphus Algotsson, bishop of Skara (1281).

D. S. nᵒ 714.

The counterseal of
Brynulphus Algotsson, bishop of Skara (1281).

D. S. nº 714.

with animal heads (Plate X). His right hand is raised in benediction and his left holds his pastoral staff, symbol of his authority. The legend reads : [† S.] BR[YNIVL]PHI. D[EI]. GRA. SCARENSIS. EPISC[OPUS] [14]). The round counterseal of Brynulphus Algotsson (40 mm.), also dating from 1281, depicts a bishop with mitre, garbed in a chasuble, holding his pastoral staff. He is kneeling before the seated Blessed Virgin holding the Divine Child, whose right hand is raised in benediction. The seal is lettered : † S. BRYNIVLPHI. DEI. GRA. SCARENSIS EPI [15]). (Plate XI)

Brynulphus died in 1317. A special office was composed in his honor and included in the early printed breviary of Skara [16]). (Plate XII)

However, the diocese of Skara is not mentioned in the deed of sale given to Emphastus as canon of Växjö and to his legitimate heirs. The house was charged with a total of 105 sol. paris. yearly rent, due to the Church of Saint-Benoît (26 sol.), Master Arnandus Provincialis (32 sol.), Johannes de Campis, burger in Paris (11 sol. 8 den.), Arnulphus as Maillez [17]) (5 sol. 10 den.), Guillelmus Canatarius [18]) (8 sol. 9 den.), and Richardus Tesson (20 sol. 10 den.). As securities, the vendors offered certain schools they possessed in Clos-Bruneau [19]).

After purchasing this house, Emphastus followed the practice of all the business-minded founders of Parisian colleges of buying up additional revenues for the support of the colleges or of their communities. On December 9, 1292, he acquired the 26 sol. paris. annual rent owned by Robertus le Coustepointier [20]) and his wife

---

14) *D. S.* I, p. 580, n⁰ 714. The deed is dated March 13, 1281.

15) *Ibid.*

16) *Bibliotheca Hagiographica Latina*, Bruxellis, 1898-1899, I, p. 221, n⁰ 1477; CHEVALIER, *Repertorium hymnologicum*, Louvain, 1892-1912, I, p. 148, n⁰ 2519; II, p. 180, n⁰ 12729; I, p. 99, n⁰ 1646; II, p. 139, n⁰ 12053; II, p. 297, n⁰ 14619; II, p. 680, n⁰ 20672; H. JOHANSSON, *Hemsjömanualet en liturgihistorisk studie*, Stockholm-Lund, 1950, p. 147; 204. For his canonization process see ANNERSTEDT, *Scriptores rerum Svecicarum*, III, 2, p. 138-185.

17) « Ernoul des maillez » (aus maillez), *travernier* living on Rue des Noyers, was taxed at 36 sol. paris. in 1296 : K. MICHAËLSSON, *Le livre de la taille de Paris l'an 1296* (Romanica Gothoburgensia n⁰ 7), Göteborg, 1958, p. 247, note 5.

18) Canetier [?]; see DU CANGE, *Gloss.*, II, 77.

19) They were adjacent on one side to the house of Petrus Roulle, beadle, and on the other side to the schools of Conrad, illuminator : M 73, n⁰ 5 [V].

20) His name is listed on the *rôle de taille* of 1292. He lived in Clos-Bruneau : A. GÉRAUD, *Paris sous Philippe-le-Bel*, Paris, 1837, p. 163.

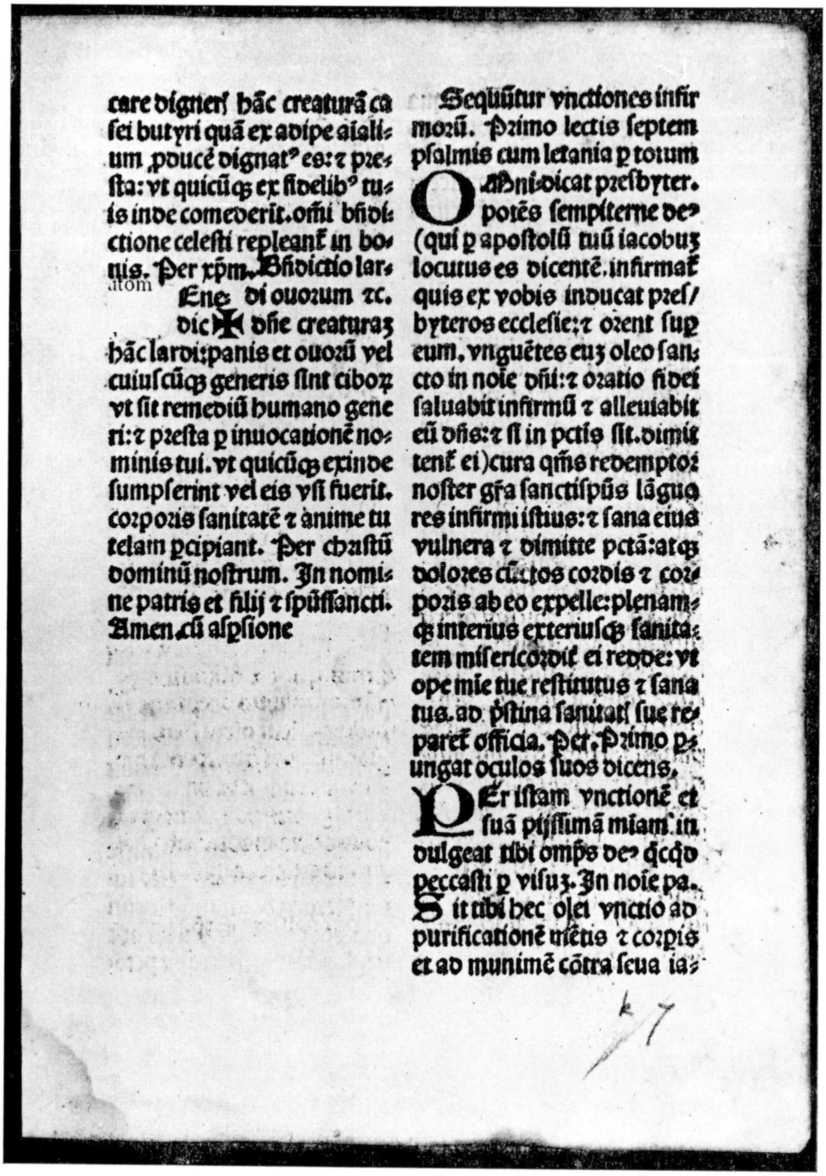

care dignter hâc creaturâ ca
sei butyri quâ ex adipe aiali-
um pducê dignat° es: t presta: vt quicûqz ex fidelib° tu-
is inde comederit. omî bñdi-
ctione celesti repleanf in bonis. Per xpm. Bñdictio lar-
di atóm Enz di ouozum tc.
dic ✠ dñe creaturaz
hâc lardi:panis et ouozu vel
cuiuscûqz generis sint ciboz
vt sit remediû humano gene-
ri:t presta p inuocatioñê no-
minis tui. vt quicûqz exinde
sumpserint vel eis vsi fuerit.
corpozis sanitatê t anime tu
telam pcipiant. Per chaistû
dominû nostrum. In nomi-
ne patris et filij t spûssancti.
Amen.cû aspsione

Sequûtur vnctiones infir
mozu. Primo lectis septem
psalmis cum letania p totum
Omni dicat presbyter.
potês sempiterne de-
(qui p apostolû tuû iacobuz
locutus es dicentê. infirmat
quis ex vobis inducat pres/
byteros ecclesie:t ozent sup
eum. vnguêtes euz oleo san-
cto in noie dñi:t ozatio fidei
saluabit infirmû t alleuiabit
eû dñs:t si in pctis sit.dimit
tenf ei)cura qñs redempto:
noster gfa sanctispûs lâguo
res infirmi istius:t sana eius
vulnera t dimitte pctâ:atqz
dolozes cûctos cordis t cor
pozis ab eo expelle:plenam-
qz interius exteriusqz sanita
tem misericozdif ei redde: vt
ope mie tue restitutus t sana
tus.ad pstina sanitatf sue re
paref officia.Per.Primo p-
ungat oculos suos dicens,
Per istam vnctionê et
suâ pijssimâ miam.in
dulgeat tibi omps de- qcqd
peccasti p visuz.In noie pa-
Sit tibi hec olei vnctio ad
purificationê mêtis t corpis
et ad munimê côtra seua ia-

PLATE XII

A page from the *Breviarium Scarense*,
Nürnberg : Georg Stachs, April 24, 1498.
Commissioned by Brynulphus Gerlaksson, bishop of Skara
(1478-1505).

Gesamtkatalog der Wiegendrucke 5458.
Yale University Rare Book Collection.

Johanna for 9 lib. paris., on a house which was located between the schools of Richard the Beadle [21]) and the schools of Guillelmus de Orvalle and from behind reached the house of Thomas Barsail [22]). Then he bought up rents on his own house; on February 4, 1293, he acquired 20 sol. and 10 den. yearly revenues from Richardus Tesson, canon of Notre-Dame [23]), probably the rents which the latter had obtained on January 3, 1284 and February 6, 1285 [24]). Emphastus paid 20 lib. Turon. for the rent. On July 19, 1298, he bought 40 sol. Turon. rent which Arnaldus de Ambella and his wife Nicolaa owned on his, that is, Emphastus', house, for which he paid 24 lib. paris. [25]).

PLATE XIII

Seal of the City of Växjö (1489).

Upsala Universitetsbibliotek.

We do not know whether Emphastus offered his house to the diocese of Skara — as Provost Andreas And did for Upsala — or whether it was acquired after his death by the canons of the Cathedral Church of Skara. The buying of revenues indicates, however, a serious endeavor to have some community of scholars in the house.

In 1292, when Emphastus bought the house in Clos-Bruneau, he was a canon of Växjö. (Plate XIII) Six years later, in 1298, he was referred to as rector of the Church [26]) of Falköping, a city

---

21) Probably Ricardus Normannus, who was the beadle of the Faculty of Theology in 1285 : *Chart. Univ. Paris.*, I, p. 628, n° 519.

22) M 73, n° 6 [VI].

23) M 73, n° 7 [VII].

24) M 73, n° 1 [I] and n° 2 [II]. Strangely enough, so far as I know, Richardus Tesson owned only 20 sol. 9 den. rents on what was to become Skara House.

25) M 73, n° 8 [VIII].

26) Was it the Church of Saint Olof, *Ecclesia S. Olvai de Phalcope Scarensis dioc.* ? Cf. B. LUNDQUIST, *Falköpings historia*, I, Falköping, 1940, p. 122.

PLATE XIV

Falköping.

After a copper engraving in
E. J. Dahlberg, *Suecia antiqua et hodierna*,
Holmiae [1667-1716], III, n⁰ 44.

approximately 20 km. south-southwest of Skara [27] (Plate XIV).
A round seal of 1441 (60 mm.) graciously portrays the three
towered-city gates (Plate XV). The legend reads : † SIGIL-
LVM † CIVITATIS † FALCOP[IEN]SIS [28]). Emphastus' title
as rector of the Church of Falköping occurs in later deeds until
around 1311, when he was for the first time called *canonicus
Scarensis* [29]) (Plate XVI).

---

27) An old view of the city can be found in E. J. DAHLBERG, *Suecia antiqua et
hodierna*. The present population of Falköping is 14,139 (census of January 1, 1960).
28) Riksarkivet, Perg. : deed of May 1, 1441.
29) M 73, n⁰ 11 [XII]; cf. *D. S.*, III, pp. 79, 81, 107, 318-319.

PLATE XV

Seal of the City of Falköping (1441).

Riksarkivet. Perg. Enlarged;
orig. 60 mm.

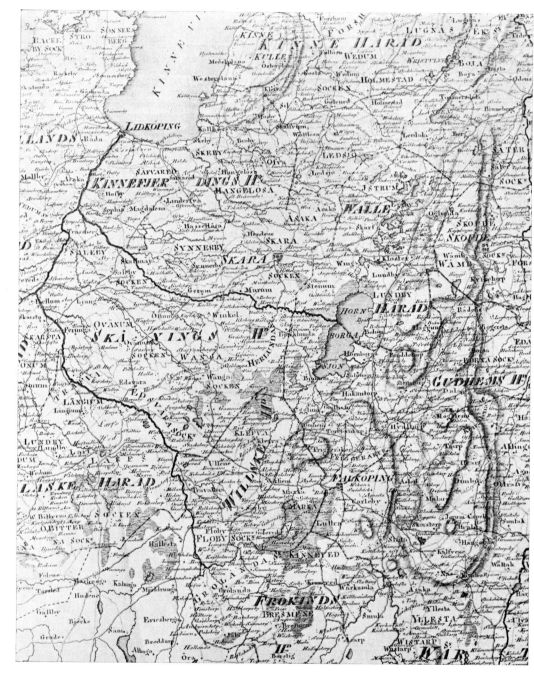

PLATE XVI Skara and Falköping as depicted on an 1807 map
of the province of Skaraborg.

Karta öfver Skaraborgs Höfdingdöme Utgifven af Friherre S. G. Hermelin.
Efter Geometriska Kartor, nyaste Astronomiska Observationer och under
Resor gjorda Rättelser; Författad af C. G. Forssell, 1807.

The oldest church in Skara, dedicated to the Blessed Virgin Mary, was founded around 1060 by Adalvard the Elder, who died in 1067 [30].

Saint Mary's Cathedral Church was nearly completed by 1130 during the bishopric of Störbjörn. It was consecrated about 1150 by Bishop Ölgrim [31].

On November 4, 1220, Pope Honorius III ordered the bishop of Skara to install regular or, if such could not be found, secular canons in the Cathedral [32].

At the end of the thirteenth century, Skara's Cathedral had a Romanesque nave and an early Gothic choir. Its outside buttresses reflect English influence; its console figures show a similarity to Norwegian Gothic. Skara's is the only cathedral in Sweden adorned with an elegent triforium, resembling that of the Cathedral of Bordeaux which was built between 1260 and 1310 during a period of intense French-Swedish cultural relations.

The architectural seal of the city *(communitas)* of Skara [33] portrays a double-towered church (1301). This may be merely a conventional representation of Saint Mary's Church. At any rate it should not be considered as the true image of the Cathedral as it was in 1301, for engravers sometimes never saw the edifice which they depicted. The seal is round and 60 mm. in size; the legend reads : † SIGILLVM. [C]IVI[TAT.] SCARENSI[?]. (Plate XVII)

Considerable rebuilding in Skara took place under Brynulphus Algotsson about the same time that Skara House was firmly established in Paris. Several donations to the Cathedral were recorded between 1305 and 1358 [34].

The religious importance of Skara is shown by the fact that several other churches were built in the city during the Middle Ages : Saint Peter, Saint Nicholas, Saint Lawrence, along with Franciscan and Dominican convents [35].

---

30) FISCHER, *Västergötlands kyrkliga konst*, p. 79.

31) *Ibid.*, p. 54.

32) *D. S.* I, p. 213, n⁰ 194.

33) Skokloster saml. n⁰ 6 : deed of May 25, 1301.

34) Dukes Erik and Waldemar donated 40 marks in 1318 (*D. S.* III, p. 345, n⁰ 2132); King Magnus and Queen Blanka contributed 100 marks in 1346 (*D. S.* V, p. 561, n⁰ 4069; III, p. 497, n⁰ 2286); H. HILDEBRAND, *Skara domkyrka*, p. 25.

35) H. SWENSSON, *Skara*, p. 42; E. SANDBERG, *Skara stads äldre gator och torg*, Skara, [1948] : M 23.

Seal of the City of Skara (1301).

Skokloster saml., nº 6. Enlarged;
orig. 65 mm.

Devotion to the Blessed Virgin Mary, the Patroness of the Cathedral, is portrayed on the 1283 seal of the Cathedral Chapter of Skara (Plate XVIII). On a round, 50 mm., seal, the Madonna is represented as seated with the Infant Jesus and accompanied by two incensing angels. The throne, decorated with the heads of animals, is somewhat similar to the one depicted on Brynulphus Algotsson's episcopal seal of 1281. The legend reads : † S. CAPITVLI ECCLES. S. MARIE CIVITAT. SCAREN. [36].

PLATE XVIII

Seal of the Chapter of
Saint Mary's Cathedral
at Skara (1283).

D. S. nº 764.

The entire Cathedral Chapter is represented on a delicately executed 70 mm. seal from 1340. The assembly of canons, each wearing his cape, is shown kneeling before a full-length effigy of the Blessed Virgin, who stands beneath a canopy with her Divine Child in her arms, surrounded by two incensing angels and symbols of the sun and the moon (Plate XIX). The legend reads : SIGILLUM † CAPITULI † E[CCLESIE † S] CARENSIS [37].

Emphastus must have been a generous and goodhearted man. In 1299 the wall between his house and that of his neighbor, Guillelmus Calot, needed repair. Though the expenses should have been divided between the two parties, Emphastus took into consideration the poverty of his neighbor and covered the expenses all by himself. Nevertheless, he made it clear that his generosity in this instance should not be interpreted to mean that in the future

---

36) *D. S.* I, p. 625, nº 764 : deed of June 24, 1283, wherein the Cathedral Chapter is referred to as *capitulum ecclesie beate virginis skaris.*

37) *D. S.* IV, p. 719, nº 3494 : deed of June 12, 1340.

PLATE XIX

Seal of the Cathedral Chapter of Skara (1340).

D. S. nᵒ 3494. Enlarged; orig. 70 mm.

either he or his successors would be obligated to pay for similar repairs [38]).

In 1300 Emphastus made an additional purchase. On August 7 he bought a small *masura* located in Rue Jocelin, or Josselin, for a yearly rent of 5 sol. paris., payable twice a year [39]) to the Church of Saint-Marcel in Paris. The Dean and the Chapter of Saint-Marcel left open to Emphastus the possibility of later buying up this rent of 5 sol. [40]).

By 1300 Emphastus' holdings in Paris consisted of a house (composed of two units) located in Clos-Bruneau and of a *masura* in Rue Josselin. But, curiously enough, on February 3, 1309, Guillelmus Bertrandi Canatarius, who held a rent of 8 sol. 9 den. paris. on part of the property of Emphastus (only on the house and not on the grange), decided to sell it, not, however, to Emphastus but to a certain tailor, Michael de Sancta-Susanna, and his wife Johanna [41]). We do not know why Emphastus did not buy this rent himself. Either Guillelmus was reluctant to sell it to him, or, what is more probable, Emphastus was no longer in Paris when this rent of 8 sol. 9 den. paris. was offered for sale.

---

38) M 73, nᵒ 9 [IX] dated September 10, 1299.

39) Two and 1/2 sol. were to be paid on the feast of Saint Remigius (October 1) and the same amount the following Easter : M 73, nᵒ 11 [X].

40) *Ibid.*

41) The price was 100 sol. paris : M 73, nᵒ 10 [XI].

VI

SUENO OF SWEDEN,
PROCTOR OF EMPHASTUS

The departure of Emphastus from Paris around 1309 seems confirmed by the fact that in 1311 he tried to buy the rent he had not acquired in 1309 from Guillelmus Bertrandi. The attempt, however, was not made by him personally but through a proctor, Sueno, a Swedish scholar studying in Paris at the time of the sale. At the order of Emphastus — who is referred to as canon of Skara — Sueno purchased, on March 31, 1311, the 8 sol. 9 den. paris. rent from Michael de Sancta-Susanna and his wife Johanna [1]. Since Emphastus is mentioned after this date only in connection with happenings in Skara itself, I surmise that he turned the ownership of the house over to the province of Skara between 1311 and 1321.

The first quarter of the fourteenth century witnessed a considerable influx of Swedish scholars to Paris. This is not surprising, since Bishop Brynulphus (1278-1317) [2] was then at the climax of his creative powers; the Cathedral of Skara was being rebuilt in French Gothic style (1312-1320) [3]. Emphastus himself, having returned to his homeland from a long sojourn in Paris, must have been instrumental in encouraging young clerics to go to Paris.

On September 16 and December 18, 1312, Emphastus is mentioned in two deeds as an arbiter in a legal case between Gudmar

---

1) M 73, n⁰ 13 [12; also marked 11, XII].

2) EUBEL, *Hierarchia Catholica* I, 438.

3) H. WIDEEN, *Skara domkyrka*, Skara, 1953, p. 8; *Lexikon für Theologie und Kirche*, IX, Freiburg im Br., 1937, p. 617, and above chapter V, note 34.

Magnusson and Bengt Johansson [Benedictus Johannis], a provost of the Cathedral Chapter of Skara. In these deeds he is always referred to as a canon of Skara [4].

The number of Swedish students in Paris around 1311-1313, during the proctorship of Sueno in Skara House, was considerable. In 1312 we find the name Thorstanus of Olandia [5]. An appeal of the University to the Pope, dated between May 6 and 11, 1313, reveals the presence of at least 15 scholars from Sweden [6] : Mag. Nicolaus de [Broghard] Broequerke, Johannes de Linköping, Laurentius de Upsalia, Mag. Henricus and Dom. Oliverus de Suessia, canons of Åbo, Johannes, presbyter, Euardus de Suessia, Nicolaus Laurentii de Suecia, Nicolaus de Suessia, Gristanus de Suessia, Laurentius Albani de Suessia, Johannes Nicolai de Suessia, Laurentius Sturberin de Suessia, Laurentius de Suessia, Philippus de Suessia, presbiter. The increase in the number of Swedish students at Paris apparently compelled Emphastus to revive his interest in the property bought in Clos-Bruneau two decades before. The house needed additional revenues. It was for this reason that he asked Sueno to act as his proctor in purchasing the rent, on March 31, 1311, for 100 sol. par. The livery of seisin was given on April 7 of the same year, by Robertus, chamberlain of Sainte-Geneviève [7].

This deed contains the last mention of Emphastus in connection with Skara House. We do not know how or when the diocese or canons of Skara acquired his house. He was still a canon of Skara in March 1317. A deed of March 16, 1317, informs us that he took part, with several other canons from Skara, in the meetings which resulted in the election of Benedictus, provost of the Cathedral

---

4) On September 16, 1312 : « Hemfastus canonicus ecclesie scarensis », *D. S.* III, p. 79, no 1867; p. 81, no 1868; p. 107, no 1896.

5) *D. S.* III, pp. 66-67, no 1851; cf. ELLEN JØRGENSEN, « Nordiske Studierejser i Middelalderen. Nordboerne ved Universitetet i Paris fra det 13. Aarhundredes Begyndelse til det 15. Aarhundredes Midte,» *Historisk Tidsskrift* [8] 5 (1915) p. 351. According to the author, eighty-five Swedish scholars visited Paris between 1300 and 1349.

6) *Chart. Univ. Paris.* II, pp. 163-165, no 703; K. KUMLIEN, « Svenskarna vid utländska Universitet under Medeltiden », *Historiska Studier tillägnade Sven Tunberg*, Uppsala, 1942, 161.

7) M 73, no 12 [XIII]. I wonder whether Emphastus' proctor, Sueno, is identical with a certain scholar Seno, mentioned among a number of Swedish subjects in the appeal of the University in 1313, but not identified as being from Sweden : *Chart. Univ. Paris.* II, p. 163, no 703, line 16.

Chapter, to the dignity of bishop of Skara [8]). On March 19, 1317, Emphastus and another canon were appointed deputies *(procuratores)* by the Chapter of Skara to negotiate in its name with the

PLATE XX

Seal of Hemphastus,
the founder of Skara House (1320).

D. S. n° 2236.

archbishop of Upsala concerning the confirmation and the consecration of the newly elected bishop of Skara [9]).

Emphastus' seal (Plate XX) was affixed to a deed of April 20, 1320, although he was not mentioned in it personally. The text suggests that he was acting in behalf of Benedictus, bishop of Skara. It is a round seal, 26 mm., with the initial of his name (H.) inscribed in the center. The legend reads : † S HEMPHASTI SACE' DOTI[S] [10]).

The next extant deed concerning the house bought by Emphastus, a *Vidimus* dated July 1, 1322 [11]), mentions neither Emphastus nor

---

8) *D. S.* III, p. 318, n° 2099.
9) *Ibid.*, III, p. 319, n° 2100.
10) *Ibid.*, III, p. 460, n° 2236.
11) M 73, n° 14 [13, XIV].

69

proctor Sueno and there is no explicit reference to the Swedish origin of the house. The provost of Paris, however, in the December 23, 1321, document copied in the *Vidimus*, calls this house the property which belongs to scholars from *Alemaigne* (« maeson qui est aus clers escoliers d'Alemaigne »). He meant Swedish students by the expression « clers escoliers d'Alemaigne, » for in the University's 1313 appeal to the Pope we find the qualification *Almani* [12]) after the names of the two Swedish scholars, the two canons from Åbo. This reference may have implied that the Swedish students belonged to the *Alemania* tribe of the English Nation of the Faculty of Arts [13]).

Furthermore, according to this deed of July 1, 1322, Pelerin de Compigne, son of Johannes de Compigne from Ivry, sold 37 sol. paris. revenues to Baudet le Flament [14]), burgher of Paris, for 16 lib. paris. [15]). From this 37 sol. paris. rent, 25 sol. 4 den. was to be received on a certain house in Clos-Bruneau that had previously belonged to Petrus Briffaut [16]) and adjoined on one side the house of Pierre Felisc [17]) and on the other the house which belonged to the « clers escoliers d'Alemaigne ». The remaining 11 sol. 8 den. yearly rent was sold on the house of Emphastus itself. The Swedish College or house of Emphastus is here identified as « meson [*sic*] des diz clers escoliers d'Alemaigne » [18]).

---

12) *Chart. Univ. Paris.* II, p. 163, n⁰ 703, line 17 : « magister Henricus et dominus Oliverus canonici Aboenses de Suessi [Suecia], *Almani*, dominus Johannes presbyter ejusdem regni, dominus Johannes de Lincopie. »

13) Boyce, *English-German Nation*, p. 28; C. Thurot, *De l'organisation de l'enseignement dans l'Université de Paris au moyen-âge*, Paris, 1850, 20; P. Kibre, *The Nations in the Mediaeval Universities* (Mediaeval Academy of America Publication n⁰ 49), Cambridge, 1948, p. 19, and passim.

14) In a 1343 *censier* of the Abbey of Sainte-Geneviève he is referred to as « feu Baudet le Flament » : Arch. Nat., S. 1626³, fol. 9 verso.

15) M 73, n⁰ 14 [13, XIV].

16) As we know from a deed of February 3, 1309, M 73, n⁰ 10 [XI], Guillelmus Bertrandi Canatarius owned 15 sol. paris. on this house, otherwise identified as neighboring that of Emphastus.

17) Pierre Felize [Felisc] of Clos Brunel paid 2 sol. to the Abbey of Saint-Geneviève in 1343 for the half of the house that belonged to « Jehanne fille, Guillaume Kalot » : Arch. Nat., S. 1626³, fol. 10 recto.

18) Previous records clearly show (cf. M 73, n⁰ 10 [XI]) that the house of Emphastus was the one neighboring that of Petrus Briffaut, and also that the house here identified as the house of the « clers escoliers d'Alemaigne » was owned previously by Guillelmus Biterne.

70

An accounting of the University of Paris (the *Computi receptarum bursarum*), made sometime between 1329 and 1336, refers to four Swedish students, Eschildus and three fellow students, living *in vico Burnelli* at that time [19]. They were most probably staying in Skara House, as there was no other Swedish property in Clos-Bruneau. The students listed as living *in vico Sancti Illarii*, Guido de Svecio and two others, were certainly inhabitants of Linköping House [20].

There is no mention of Skara House in the 1343 and 1365 *censiers* of the Abbey of Saint-Geneviève [21].

---

19) *Chart. Univ. Paris.* II, p. 661-662, n° 1184.

20) *Ibid.*, p. 661, n° 1184; cf. Schück, *op. cit.*, 53. Among the Swedish scholars who lived in Paris around 1327 was Thomas de Suecia « loco rectoris » : *Chart. Univ. Paris.* II, p. 296, n° 859. He cannot be identified — as was done by editors of *Auct.* I — with Thomas Haquini de Orabro, who was only *determinans* in 1339 : *Auct.* I, 27, 37.

21) Arch. Nat., S. 1626³, fol. 9 verso — 10 recto; S. 1626⁴, fol. 8 recto; 13 verso; 32 recto; 57 verso; 67 recto.

VII

PROVOST BRYNULPHUS « DE SCARENCE »,

« ESCOLIER ESTUDIANT A PARIS »

The first notable Swedish scholar from the diocese of Skara in Paris after Emphastus and Suenonus was Brynulphus Karlsson (Brunyulphus, Bryniulphe, Brunulphus Karoli), provost « en l'église cathedral de Scarence, ou royaume de Suece, maistre es ars, escolier estudiant a Paris » [1]). He took upon himself the care of the almost a hundred year old house in Clos-Bruneau.

His name first appeared in the *Liber procuratorum* of the English-German Nation in 1379, when he became bachelor of Arts under Master Gerardus de Kalkar with a *bursa* of 5 sol. 6 den. [2]). A year later he was *licentiatus* under Master Jordanus de Clivis with the much higher *bursa* of 8 sol. [3]). (Such an increase was usually a sign of improved financial conditions.) He obtained the *magisterium* in 1380 under Master Johannes Luberti [4]), and paid the customary 1 franc for *jucundus introitus*, together with his countryman Hermannus Everhardi de Swecia [5]). On May 5, 1382, Brynulphus was elected proctor of the English Nation, but refused to accept the office. He paid, however, the customary 1 franc which a proctor was supposed to contribute when elected for the first time. As a good and tradition-loving member of his Nation, he

---

1) M 73, n° 15 [14, XV].

2) *Auct.* I, 573, 37; A. Budinszky, *op. cit.*, p. 218.

3) *Ibid.*, I, 588, 18.

4) *Ibid.*, I, 588, 45.

5) *Ibid.*, I, 589, 42.

participated in the dinner following the election, in a tavern called *Ad habitum Gilleti* [6].

Like Emphastus, Brynulphus also was ready to help the needy. When Master Radulphus de Lübeck became sick and needed support, the compassionate provost of Skara loaned him 8 francs on July 13, 1382. A Bible was offered as security [7]. Radulphus agreed to pay the money back by Christmas, and consented, if this condition were not met, to the sale of the Bible by the Nation to compensate Brynulphus [8]. When, as might be expected, the money was not returned by Christmas, Brynulphus on January 13, 1383, requested the Nation to put the Bible up for sale. His Christian charity had made him forget the advice given by Pseudo-Boethius in the *Disciplina scholarium,* that circumspection in lending money may save later resentment [9]. On April 1, 1383, Brynulphus was still waiting for the repayment of the loan; finally he asked that the Bible be sold for a price which he left to the discretion of the University.

PLATE XXI

Seal of
Brynulphus Karlsson,
provost of Skara (1397).

R. P. B. 2868.

Brynulphus needed the money because he was thinking of buying back the 11 sol. 8 den. yearly revenue on the property of the Swedish scholars, the former house of Emphastus, revenue which had been sold a half century before, on July 1, 1322, to Baudet le Flament [10].

Unfortunately, we do not have all the deeds referring to this

---

6) *Ibid.,* I, 621, 13.
7) *Ibid.,* I, 623, 39.
8) *Ibid.,* I, 645, 10.
9) Migne, *Patrologia Latina,* 64, 1231C.
10) M 73, nº 14 [13, XIV].

purchase by Brynulphus, but the livery of seisin given by Jehan Noël, canon and chamberlain [11]) of Sainte-Geneviève, dated June 19, 1385, informs us that the 11 sol. 8 den. revenue, now acquired by Brynulphus, had been previously received by Perrenelle la Riche, wife of the late Estienne le Riche, who lived in Rue du-Mont-Saint-Hilaire. The sale was effectuated by Simon l'Alemant [12]), acting as proctor for the said Perrenelle, who sold the 11 sol. 8 den. revenue on the house of the Swedish scholars to the « honorable home maistre Bryniulphe » for 12 lib. Turon. [13]).

Brynulphus must have left Paris a few years after the purchase, for his name appears for the last time in the 1385 livery of seisin. From then on, the house was referred to as belonging to the canons of the Church of Skara or to the « province of Sweden » [14]).

Brynulphus Karlsson's seal, used in his capacity as provost of the Skara Cathedral Chapter in 1397 (Plate XXI), retains possibly something of the tradition of the English-German Nation in Paris. On his round, 25 mm. seal, Brynulphus is represented garbed in canonical cape, kneeling before the effigy of a saint; the Gothic-lettered legend reads : S BRYNIULPHI KAROLI [15]). I am rather inclined to identify this saint with Saint Catherine, as she seems to be holding a wheel in her right hand and a palm in her left. The English-German Nation, of which Brynulphus Karlsson was an outstanding member in Paris, held Saint Catherine in special reverence, and she was portrayed on their seal [16]).

---

11) Cf. Bibl. Sainte-Geneviève, Ms. 369 (E. f. in fol. 11) : *Cens, rentes et fonds de terre deubs à l'office des pitances et cuisinne de l'esglise Sainte-Geneviève ou Mont de Paris*, fol. 74 verso : « En l'an 1377, fu ce livre commencié en papier par Mess. Jehan Noel, qui pour lors estoit pitancier. » CH. KOHLER, *Catalogue des manuscrits de la Bibliothèque Sainte-Geneviève*, Paris, 1893, I, p. 230.

12) Simon owned a house, later called the house of Saint-Yves, in Clos-Bruneau around 1380 : BERTY, *Topographie*, VI, p. 100.

13) M 73, n° 15 [14, XV].

14) « Spectat ad illos qui sunt canonici in ecclesia Scharensi in Zwesia » : *Auct.* I, 754, 20; « spectabat ad provinciam Zwesie » : *ibid.*, 754, 20.

15) RPB. 2868 : deed of March 31, 1397.

16) R. GANDILHON, *Sigillographie des universités de France*, Paris, 1952, p. 90, n° 111, Pl. XIV.

VIII

ABSENCIA SCOLARUM

During Brynulphus' stay in Paris, the number of Swedish scholars studying in Paris decreased considerably. According to the records at our disposal, during the prosperous years of 1340-1370 more than 40 students were registered in various faculties, but in the years Brynulphus spent in Skara House, 1380-85, we can find only five scholars mentioned in the official registers [1].

The diocese of Skara was hardly in a financial position to send students to Paris. Its territory had suffered greatly during the Danish and Norwegian invasions, Saint Mary's Cathedral itself having been burned down in 1380 [2].

In April 1392, because of a total absence of students, the three houses which were properties of the scholars from the Northern regions, the *Domus Dacie*, the house of *Cornu Cervi* [the College of Linköping], and the house « de ymaginis nostre Domine in vico Brunelli » were turned over to the Nation following upon a decision made by the rector of the University [3]. This is the first time in existing records that the House of Skara is identified as the House « with the sign *Nostre Domine* ».

---

1) They are Henricus Magni de Suecia, 1379-80 (*Auct.* I, 572, 27; 593, 29); Henricus Andree de Svecia, 1389 (*Auct.* I, 773, 10); Hermannus Everardi de Swecia, 1380-82 (*Auct.* I, 584, 34); Bero Gregorii de Suecia, 1380 (*Auct.* I, 587, 12); Andreas Johannis de Swecia, 1382 (*Auct.* I, 617, 24); cf. L. Daae, *Matrikler over Nordiske Studerende ved fremmede Universiteter*, Christiania, 1885.

2) « A Dacis et Noricis fere tota Westgocia fuit vastata, ac Civitas Scharensis cum Ecclesia Cathedrali et Junacopia, per incendium perierunt » : E. M. Fant, ed., *Scriptores rerum Suecicarum medii aevi*, Upsalia, 1818, I, 45; A. Romdahl - S. Dahlgren, *Skara domkyrkas byggynadshistoria*, pp. 42-43.

3) *Auct.* I, 661, 27 ss.

Immediately after the decision of the rector, the Nation appointed a committee, composed of the representatives of the provinces of the English-German Nation, to take care of the rents and revenues of the House [4].

The action of the University in turning the three houses over to the Nation was entirely justified, for practically no Swedish students are reported studying in Paris between 1385 and 1395. The House of Skara, now called *Ad Imaginem Nostre Domine*, was badly in need of repairs [5]. On March 24, 1392, the Nation reappointed the same committee to take adequate action [6]. Some repairs were made by February 1394, when the work was viewed by an impressive group of masters [7].

The renting of the house was left to the receptor. He reported, on July 22, 1397, receiving 34 francs 11 sol. 8 den. paris. revenues [8]. By this time the House of Skara was in even greater need of immediate repairs : the roof was falling down and one room was in miserable condition. The Nation, instead of starting small and local repairs, tried to get additional money to make the whole house acceptable and habitable [9].

---

4) The province of Scotland was represented by the receptor, a Scotchman; *Almania inferior*, by EGIDIUS JUTFAES; *Almania superior*, by GEORGIUS RAIN : *Auct.* I, 662, 16.

5) *Auct.* I, 678, 28; 35.

6) *Ibid.*, I, 676, 35.

7) *Ibid.*, I, 688, 9.

8) *Ibid.*, I, 744-745.

9) *Ibid.*, I, 745, 10.

IX

LEGITIMATE CLAIMANTS

FROM SKARA

There were only a few Swedish students at Paris from 1385 to 1395. After 1395 their number increased. On August 1, 1397, Ruthgerus (Rogerus) Trost de Swecia requested the *domus de Swecia* in Clos-Bruneau for himself and for his fellow scholars [1]. But the legalistically minded Nation did not hurry its decision. By now it knew that the house *in vico Brunelli* was not its property, but was in doubt as to whether the house belonged 1) to those who were from Sweden, or 2) to one Swedish province, or 3) to a certain *collegium*. (« *Collegium* » probably means a collegiate chapter of canons) [2]. But by January 7, 1398, the Nation knew that the house belonged to the canons of the Church of Skara. Therefore, since anyone who wanted to occupy the house had to prove that he was a canon of the Skara Cathedral Chapter, Ruthgerus, realizing he had no legal claim on the house, declared that he would withdraw his request.

By the beginning of January 1398, a rightful claimant had appeared, in the person of Aquinus Asari [3], provost of the Cathedral Church of Skara (Plate XXII), who several times presented

---

1) *Auct.* I, 746, 6.

2) *Ibid.*, I, 746, 8-11.

3) Håkan Azersson, Haquinus Azeri or Aceri, Haquon, Hacon, *D. S. n. s.* I, p. 275, nº 362; p. 494, nº 649, note 3; p. 496, nº 652. *Ibid.*, II, p. 319, nº 1329; p. 332, nº 1347; p. 404, nº 1445; p. 661, nº 1739. His 31 mm. round seal, dating from 1405, portrays a bearded Saint Andrew on a cross. Håkan's coat of arms is barely visible beneath the feet of the apostle : *D. S. n. s.* I, p. 494, nº 649.

his claim to the house [4]). The Nation did not take any action but referred him to the University, because it was from the University that the Nation had received the house in trusteeship. Since the provost from Skara pressed his claim, the Nation finally agreed to

PLATE XXII

Seal of Håkan Azersson (Aquinus Asari),
archdeacon of Skara (1405).

Svensk Diplomatarium, C. Silfverstolpe, ed.
[henceforth referred to as *D. S. n. s.*] n° 649.

support his claim before the University under four conditions : the provost 1) would not alienate the house without the consent of the Nation; 2) would not admit any fellow scholar from the province of Skara into the house without the consent of the Nation; 3) would, if he should leave Paris, return the house to the Nation [5]) ; 4) would within a year prove that he was a member of the Cathedral Chapter

---

4) *Auct.* I, 754, 23; February 9, 1398 : *ibid.,* 758, 38. Johannes Mullinger de Austria, Egidius de Jutfaes, a longtime expert on the house of Skara (cf. in 1392, *Auct.* I, 662, 17), and Galterus Forestarii were appointed deputies to negotiate with the archdeacon of Skara : *Ibid.,* I, 759, 37.

5) *Ibid.,* I, 755, 19.

of Skara. The Nation also asked him to give a pledge, in writing, sealed by his own seal, that he would not make any repairs without its permission and that he would spend the revenues of the house on repairs, not keep them for himself — annoying conditions that had certainly not been foreseen by Emphastus, the benefactor of the Cathedral Chapter of the Church of Skara [6].

The Nation was not in a good bargaining position. On March 13, 1398, it was reported to the Nation that the tenants were not paying rent for the building. Urged on by the provost and discouraged by the miserable condition of the house, the Nation, on July 28, 1398, recognized the claims of Aquinus Asari *in principio*. Once in possession of the house, the provost asked for the rents, but the Nation refused them [7].

On April 3, 1399, Aquinus Asari dispelled any remaining legal difficulties by showing the *procuratorium* given by the bishop of Skara which made him procurator of the House. Aquinus Asari was appointed superior of the House, and a copy of the *procuratorium* was handed over to the Nation [8].

Now that he was in possession of the house, Aquinus Asari claimed the rents previously received by the Nation [9]. As was always the case whenever money was to be paid out, the Nation was not in a hurry to act. Deputies were appointed to examine the records of the Nation, and the Nation complained about the absence of masters who could remember all the details concerning the renting of the House of Skara [10]. The Nation, three years later, was still putting off the payment, ingenuously appointing new committees to look over the records for any debts the Nation might owe to the archdeacon of Skara [11].

It is no wonder that the archdeacon, with no payment coming in from the Nation, could not carry out the necessary repairs. The

---

6) *Ibid.*, I, 762, 3-16; 763, 1-5.

7) *Ibid.*, I, 769, 6; 771, 35; 780, 25. Among the tenants were a certain Johannes Tungern, who lived in Skara House before 1399 and left it in a disastrous condition (*Auct.* I, 793, 38), and Jordanus de Derthesen, a newly promoted master of Arts, who was living in the House in 1399 (*ibid.*, 792, 36 and cf. 775, 26).

8) *Ibid.*, I, 792, 44; 793, 12; 796, 22; 799, 1.

9) *Ibid.*, I, 780, 25.

10) *Ibid.*, I, 818, 10-35; 819, 11.

11) *Ibid.*, I, 821, 13; also in K. H. KARLSSON ed., *Svenskt Diplomatarium, Supplement [1401-1420]*, IV, Stockholm, 1903-1904 [henceforth referred to as *D. S.* IV], p. 1, n° 2846.

house had fallen into so dilapidated a condition that the neighbors were carrying away the stones. The archdeacon's complaints against a certain Thomas Fabri resulted in no positive action except the usual appointment of a committee [12]; the final outcome could be summed up in the words of the Nation : *non fecerunt aliquid in illo facto* [13]. The patience of Aquinus Asari ran out by August 17, 1401. On this day he announced his intention of leaving Paris and substituted two proctors for the government of the House : Navno Johannis de Dacia [14] who was to become the bishop of Västerås and subsequently of Odense, and Christianus Hemmingi [15], later bishop of Ribe. The last words of the departing archdeacon of Skara addressed to the Nation reminded it to repay the money it owed to the *Domus Scarensis* [16]. Aquinus Asari (Håkan Azersson) was back in Sweden on July 22, 1403 [17].

In the meantime, the bishop and the Chapter were busily engaged in the rebuilding of Saint Mary's Cathedral, which had been destroyed by fire in 1380. On February 9, 1402, Pope Boniface IX

---

12) *Auct.* I, 828, 17; *D. S.* IV, p. 22, nᵒ 2370; *Auct.* I, 829, 45; *D. S.* IV, p. 30, nᵒ 2880.

13) *Auct.* I, 830, 7.

14) Navno (Nafno, Nawne) Johannis (Krigebusk), son of Jens Gyrsting, a judge (JØRGENSEN, « Nordiske Studierejser i Middelalderen », *Historisk Tidsskrift*, 8ᵈᵉ Raekke 5 [1915] 365); bachelor of Arts from Paris in 1398 under Ruthgerus de Svecia (*Auct.* I, 763, 28); lic. and *incipiens* in 1399, paying 8 sol. bursas (*ibid.*, I, 799, 30, 32). Elected proctor of the English Nation on June 2, 1401 (*ibid.*, 828, 36). Left Paris around 1403, became canon of Lund, and on Sept. 12, 1414, a *baccal. decretorum*, was appointed bishop of Västerås (Arosiensis) (EUBEL, I, 109; *D. S. n. s.* I, p. 58, nᵒ 2112, etc. p. 695). On July 14, 1421, he was transferred to the seat of Odense (GAMS, 331; EUBEL, I, 382). He died in 1440.

15) Christiern Hemmingi (Hemmingsen) was born in 1378 in Seeland. In 1401 he was already in Paris (*Auct.* I, 832, 3, 37). On Nov. 8, 1404, mentioned as provost of Roskilde (KR. ERSLEV - W. CHRISTENSEN - A. HUDE, *Danmarks Breve fra Middelalderen* [Repertorium Diplomaticum Regni Danici Mediaevalis] København, 1899, III, p. 47, nᵒ 4656; *D. S. n. s.* II, p. 452, nᵒ 1511); Oct. 7, 1418, appointed bishop of Ribe, suffr. of Lund (GAMS, 331; EUBEL, I, 421; *Rep. Dipl. Regni Danici*, III, p. 282, nᵒ 5905; J. LANGEBEK - P. F. SUHM, *Scriptores Rerum Danicarum Medii Aevi*, Hauniae, 1792, VII, p. 407); later King Erik's envoy to the Council of Basel. He died Jan. 21, 1455 (P. ENGELSTOFT - S. DAHL, *Dansk Biografisk Leksikon*, København, 1936, vol. X, p. 52).

16) *Auct.* I, 831, 43; 832, 19; *D. S.* IV, p. 31, nᵒ 2883.

17) *D. S. n. s.* I, p. 275, nᵒ 362. He is mentioned several times as archdeacon of Skara : 1405, Oct. 23, *ibid.*, p. 494, nᵒ 649, note 3; Oct. 25, *ibid.*, p. 496, nᵒ 652; 1406, Sept. 9, *ibid.*, p. 585, nᵒ 679; 1410, July 9, *D. S. n. s.* II, p. 319, nᵒ 1347; 1411, June 29, *ibid.*, p. 404, nᵒ 1445; and 1413, June 29, *ibid.*, p. 661, nᵒ 1739.

PLATE XXIII

Panel on a stall in the choir
of the mediaeval Cathedral of
Skara. Woodcarving represent-
ing an ape gazing intra mirror
as a symbol of worldly vanity,
and a dog, symbol of watch-
fulness.

Västergötlands Museum, Skara.

spoke of the splendid but unfinished edifice of the Cathedral of Skara, which urgently needed the help of the faithful to be completed [18]. (Plate XXIII)

On December 19, 1406, Gregory XII in his letter to Brynulphus, bishop of Skara and former Paris scholar, expressed his regret that the latter and the canons of Skara were lacking the necessary funds for the reconstruction of the Cathedral [19]. It is not surprising, then, that the Cathedral Chapter could not afford to spend money on the reconstruction of another property, namely the Skara House in Paris [20].

The Nation, though most delinquent in satisfying its own financial obligation to the owners of Skara House, felt no embarrassment in asking for a written assurance from the newly appointed proctors that they would not give the house to anyone without its consent [21]. The proctors, however, on December 31, 1401, announced that they intended to leave the *Domus Scarensis* and proposed Jacobus de Haarlem [22] and Hermannus de Dacia for proctors and governors, probably because no Swedish students were in Paris at that time [23].

But one of the proctors either did not leave or came back shortly; on June 26, 1403, Navno Johannis de Dacia gave the Nation an accounting of the financial status of Skara House, here identified as *Ad Imaginem Nostre Domine*. At the same time he asked the Nation to accept Michael de Dacia as his substitute [24]. The accounts revealed 18 francs of profit on the House. This money was left in the hands of the two proctors, Jacobus de Haarlem and Michael de

---

18) « ... ecclesia Scharensis sumptuoso et pregrandi edificio inchoata et nondum consumata existit, que non modica sumptuosa indigere noscatur subuentione » *D. S. n. s.* IV, p. 55, nº 2906.

19) « ... ecclesia Scarensis dudum ignis incendio destructa fuerat et reparatione non modica indigere noscebatur ad quam episcopi Scarensis existentis pro tempore et dilectorum canonicorum ipsius ecclesie proprie non sufficiebant facultates » *D. S. n. s.* IV, p. 229, nº 3128.

20) The Cathedral was completed during the bishopric of Sven Grotte (1436-1449), who founded the Corpus Christi and Saint Eric chapels : A. ROMDAHL - S. DAHLGREN, *Skara domkyrkas byggnadshistoria*, 41-45.

21) August 26, 1401 : *Auct.* I, 832, 32; *D. S.* IV, p. 32, nº 2884.

22) Jacobus Johannis de Haarlem, determinans in 1396 : *Auct.* I, 718, 35; licentiatus 1397 : *ibid.*, 741, 25, and magister. Proctor of the English-German Nation several times in 1402 : *ibid.*, 838, 4; 842, 3; 850, 47. Cf. *ibid.*, 975, col. 1.

23) *Auct.* I, 837, 25. Fredericus Traest is the last (Spring, 1400) we know of, before 1401 : *ibid.*, I, 815, 23.

24) *Ibid.*, I, 860, 20; 861, 16.

Dacia [25]). But the new proctor, Jacobus, was not very eager later on to give an accounting to the Nation [26]). On January 24, 1405, he resigned from his proctorship, appointing as his successor Henricus de Dinteren [27]). Jacobus was given a year to repay whatever he owed to the Nation for Skara House. On February 22, 1405, he reported that his expenses concerning the House amounted to 20 francs, 13 sol. and 6 den. and the revenues to 36 francs; therefore a debit of 15 francs, 2 sol. and 6 den. remained [28]).

---

25) *Ibid.*, I, 860, 40.

26) *Ibid.*, I, 885, 25; *D. S.* IV, p. 152, n⁰ 3025; *Auct.* I, 886, 20.

27) *Ibid.*, I, 893, 25; *D. S.* IV, p. 158, n⁰ 3033. Henricus de Dinteren, determinans in 1400 under Mag. Wilhelmus Bloc : *Auct.* I, 810, 21; licentiatus and mag. in 1401 : *ibid.*, 826, 34; 827, 18. Proctor of the English-German Nation 1405, December 16 : *ibid.*, 913, 12. On April 25, 1406, requested a letter of introduction to a master in Montpellier : *ibid.*, 920, 44.

28) *Ibid.*, I, 896, 15; *D. S.* IV, 161, n⁰ 3037.

X

SKARA HOUSE RENTED TO
BEADLE BOEMUNDUS

After the departure of Aquinus Asari, there were no Swedish students living in Skara House. The tenants did not care about the upkeep. On February 19, 1405, the Nation was informed that the house was ruined : the roof was falling down and the building was so filthy « that even pagans would not live in it » [1]. Several times it was decided to proceed to repair the house. To cover the expenses, the Nation counted first on the money owed by Jacobus de Haarlem, the former governor of Skara House *(Ad Imaginem Nostre Domine)*; secondly, the Nation expressed its readiness to invest the 36 francs the Nation itself owed to the House [2]; thirdly, it decided to negotiate a loan from the beadle, Boemundus [3].

October 4, 1405, arrived and the Nation still lacked the needed funds to carry out the projected repairs. It was decided, therefore, that the southern half of the house, half of the cellar, the garden, and the stable be turned over to Boemundus [4], the beadle of the

---

1) *Auct.* I, 895, 27 : « ruinosa, caduca et valde male cooperta et fetida, ymo in tantum quod non vellent domum pagani ».

2) *Auct.* I, 895, 6; *D. S.* IV, p. 160, nᵒ 3035; *Auct.* I, 895, 37; *D. S.* IV, p. 160, nᵒ 3036; cf. *Auct.* I, 896, 45; *D. S.* IV, p. 162, nᵒ 3039; *Auct.* I, 903, 18.

3) July 22, 1405 : *Auct.* I, 903, 48; 904, 7; *D. S.* IV, p. 172, nᵒ 3053. Cf. September 21 : *Auct.* I, 905, 10; *D. S.* IV, p. 180, nᵒ 3058.

4) Boemundus Theodorici de Lutrea [Kaiserslautern in Pfalz], from the diocese of Trier, was elected major beadle in 1392 : *Auct.* I, 661, note 1; he held this office for more than sixty years. He died in 1453, leaving his house « ad intersignum Sancti Michaelis », which he had bought from Oliverius de Imperio in 1415, to the English-German Nation : *Chart. Univ. Paris.* IV, p. 299, nᵒ 2042. The house was located in Clos-Bruneau, very near to Skara House.

Nation, during his lifetime. In return, Boemundus would bind himself to spend 50 francs for repair. A yearly amount of 4 or 5 francs would in lieu of rent be deducted from the Nation's debt of 50 francs. After receiving the equivalent of 50 francs in rent, Boemundus was to pay 4 or 5 francs each year for rent until the end of his life [5]. If students from Sweden should return, they were to live in the part of the house which was towards the College of Beauvais (the northern part). Boemundus was authorized, on December 27, 1405, to put up the northern part for rent until legitimate students should claim the house. The minutes of this agreement were transcribed into an official deed and sealed with the great seal of the Nation [6].

---

5) *Auct.* I, 908, 35 — 909, 36; *D. S.* IV, p. 181-82, nº 3060.

6) *Auct.* I, 913, 25; *D. S.* IV, p. 197, nº 3078. Very soon a tenant appeared. The rent was priced at 8 francs from October 4, 1405, to June 24, 1406 : *Auct.* I, 909, 29. On December 27, 1405, the Nation still owed 5 francs to the roofmaker. It was decided to press the former proctor of Skara House for the repayment of his debts : *Auct.* I, 913, 32-37.

The deed of agreement between Boemundus and the Nation concerning Skara House may be the document recorded as being kept in the *archa* of the English-German Nation and listed in the inventory of the properties of the Nation : « Instrumentum de reparacionibus factis in collegio de *cornu cervi* et [*domus ad ymaginem Nostre Domine*] » : *Auct.* II, 320, 4-5.

XI

SIGGO UDDSSON AND THE STATUTES
OF SKARA HOUSE

It seems that the election of one of the former proctors of Skara House, Brynulphus Karlsson, to the episcopal seat of Skara [1]) increased the interest among Swedish scholars in their House in Paris.

Brynulphus' predecessor, Thorstanus, who became bishop of Skara on April 13, 1391, had resigned; Brynulphus must have acted as administrator before his official appointment on March 23, 1405 [2]). His 40 mm. round episcopal seal, dating from 1402 (Plate XXIV), portrays a standing Madonna holding the Divine Child. Brynulphus Karlsson kneels before her in episcopal attire, mitered and with pastoral staff, his coat of arms at his feet. The group is covered by an arch. The legend reads : SECRETV BRYNIVL[PHI] DEI GRA EPI SCAREN [3]).

On February 14, 1406, Siggo (Ziggo, Sigge) Uddsson (Odonis, Otson, Odzssons), canon of Skara, appeared before the Nation and unhesitatingly asked for the accounts of the House and for permission to take it over [4]). The Nation, as in similar cases, tried to gain

---

1) 1405, March 23, 1424, June 5 : EUBEL, I, 438-439; BUDINSZKY, *op. cit.*, 218.

2) On July 22, 1404, Thorstanus refers to him as *prepositus et coadiutor* : *D. S. n. s.* I, p. 356, n⁰ 468.

3) *D. S. n. s.* I, p. 163, n⁰ 227, note 1. Deed of September 9, 1402.

4) Siggo on October 23, 1405 was still in Sweden : *D. S. n. s.* I, 495, n⁰ 651; *Auct.* II, 3, 26; 6, 4; *D. S.* IV, 239, n⁰ 3138. Siggo Uddsson was the son of Udd Matsson and Ingrid Karlsdotter and the grandson of Mats Uddsson, who married Ingeborg Knutsdotter around 1331 : K. G. LUNDHOLM, « Vinstorpaätten och släkter med denna

time. As first condition for any further negotiations, it requested the incorporation of Siggo into the *provincia Almanie* [5]).

But Siggo was a jurist and a student in Canon Law in Paris. He knew how to proceed in litigation. After his incorporation into the *provincia Almanie* on April 7, 1407, he asked for the deed of agreement between Boemundus and the Nation concerning Skara House [6]). On May 14 of the same year, Siggo worked out an agreement with Jacobus Haarlem, former proctor of the House, and very soon afterwards the property in Clos-Bruneau was again in the hands of the canons of Skara [7]).

PLATE XXIV

Seal of
Brynulphus Karlsson,
bishop of Skara (1402).

D. S. n. s. nº 227.

Siggo Uddsson learned from the case of Nicolaus Skrilvara, of which we have written in Chapter III dealing with the College of Linköping. While he asked, on March 13, 1407, for the same arbitrators who had settled the dispute between the dean of Linköping and the Nation, namely for Pierre Cauchon and Oliverius de Imperio, he nevertheless seems to have brought his negotiations to an end without the interference of any arbitrators. Although he was somewhat slower than his compatriot from Linköping, Nicolaus Skrilvara, he conducted his case with much more firmness and competense. Thanks to his tact and legal experience he successfully surmounted the delaying tractics of the Nation.

ätts vapen», *Äldre Svenska Frälsesläkter*, I, 1. (1957) 103. Siggo's brother, Karl Uddsson, was dean of Skara : *D. S. n. s.* III, p. 404, nº 2570.

5) *Auct.* II, 6, 29.

6) C. ANNERSTEDT, *Upsala Universitets Historia (1477-1654)*, Upsala, 1877, p. 7, note 6; p. 9, note 2; *Auct.* II, 11, 22.

7) *Auct.* II, 13, 44.

Siggo's first task was to organize the House. Blessed with qualities which later made him an excellent bishop [8]), he realized that order and discipline had to be maintained if Skara House was not to fall into ruins again; consequently, he composed certain Statutes or rules of conduct for the members of the quasi-Collegium. These Statutes, composed around 1407, were intended to govern the life of the scholars living in the House of the Church of Skara *(Ad Imaginem Nostre Domine)* [9]). Siggo signed the Statutes as proctor, which term, according to the terminology of other Northern Statutes, those of Upsala, designated the superior of the House.

Beside Siggo, there was, according to Schück [10]), only one scholar from Sweden in Skara House, namely Gunno Andree [11]), a former student at Prague. The others who signed the Statutes were Henninghus Rocstede [12]) and Henricus Everardi de Yselstein [13]).

The Statutes, composed of thirteen paragraphs, were shorter than those of the College of Upsala [14]) and seem to have been written by Siggo Uddsson himself. They reveal his solicitude for discipline, fraterna l help, and charity. (Plate XXV)

★

---

8) 1424, June 5 - 1435, December 31 : EUBEL, I, 439; II, 232; ANNERSTEDT, *op. cit.*, p. 7, note 6.

9) Original in Arch. Nat. M 73, n⁰ 16 [15, XVI]; edited in *Auct.* II, Intr. pp. xi-xii.

10) SCHÜCK, *op. cit.*, 75.

11) Gunne Andersson Prika is mentioned on December 10, 1413 as canon of Skara : *D. S. n. s.* II, p. 742, n⁰ 1855; also on July 5, 1414 : *ibid.*, p. 832, n⁰ 1979; on July 20, 1415 : *D. S. n. s.* III, p. 60, n⁰ 2113. He enrolled at the University of Prague in 1397 under Petrus Slewyng, rector, and paid 14 gr. From there he went to Paris, where he lived in Skara House around 1407 : *Monumenta Historica Universitatis Carolo-Ferdinandeae Pragensis*, Praguae, 1834, II, 1, p. 148; *Auct.* II, Intr., p. xii.

12) A certain Hemming i Rökstada is mentioned on May 21, 1414, as living in Sweden : *D. S. n. s.* II, p. 812.

13) A diary of Vadstena refers to a certain Dominus Tyrrerus who returned in 1406 from Paris with several books he had bought there, namely a *Catholicon*, a *Dictionarium*, the *Speculum Historiale*, and a *Racionale divinorum officiorum*. He donated all these books to the monastery of Vadstena. There is, however, no explicit mention to the effect that Tyrrerus actually studied at the University of Paris. He may have been only a visitor in Paris : E. M. FANT, *Scriptores rerum Svecicarum*, I, 1, p. 121-22.

14) Dated April 23-28, 1291 : *D. S.* I, pp. 119-123, n⁰ 1045.

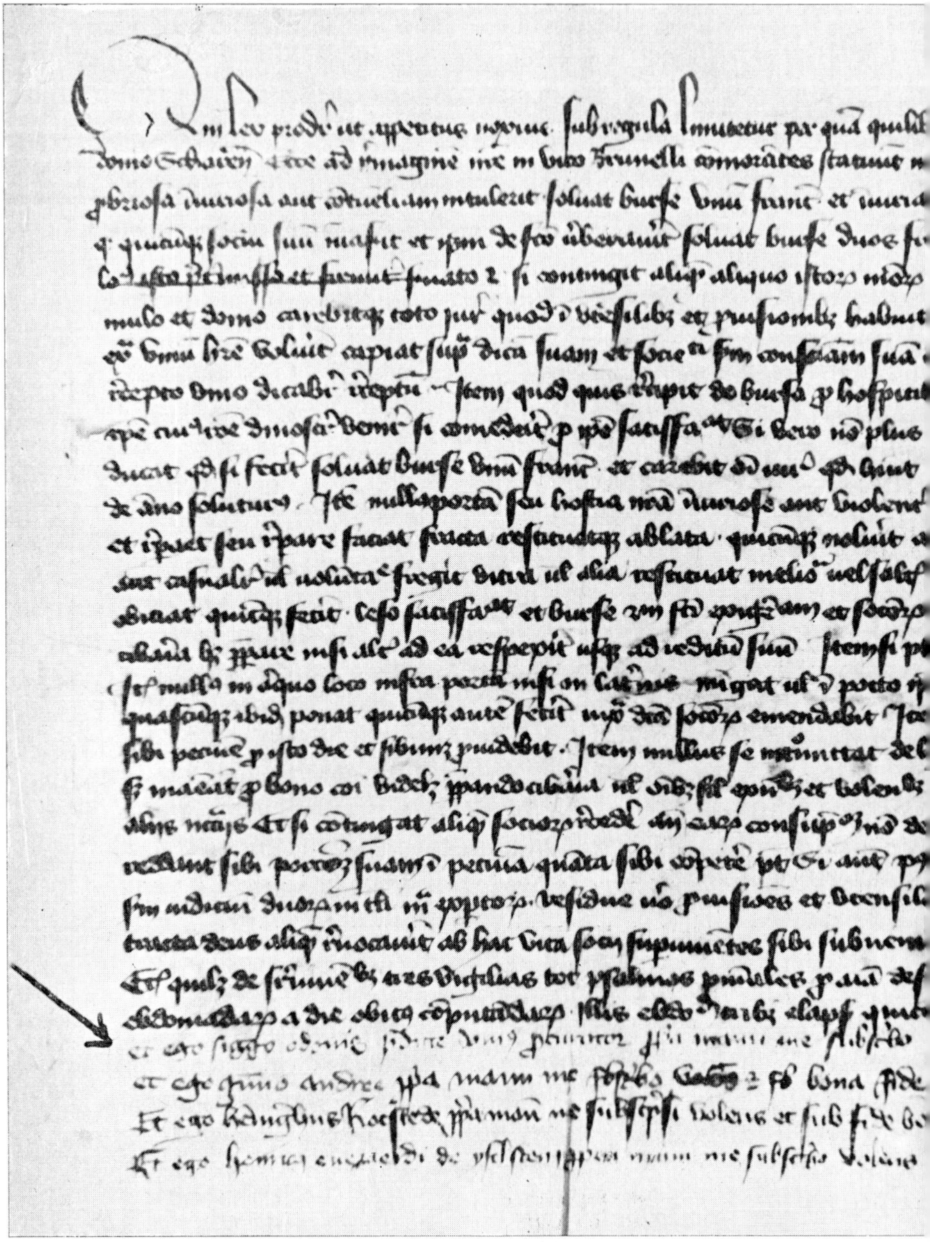

PLATE XXV

Statutes of the commun
Arrow points to the signature
rator of Skara House (la

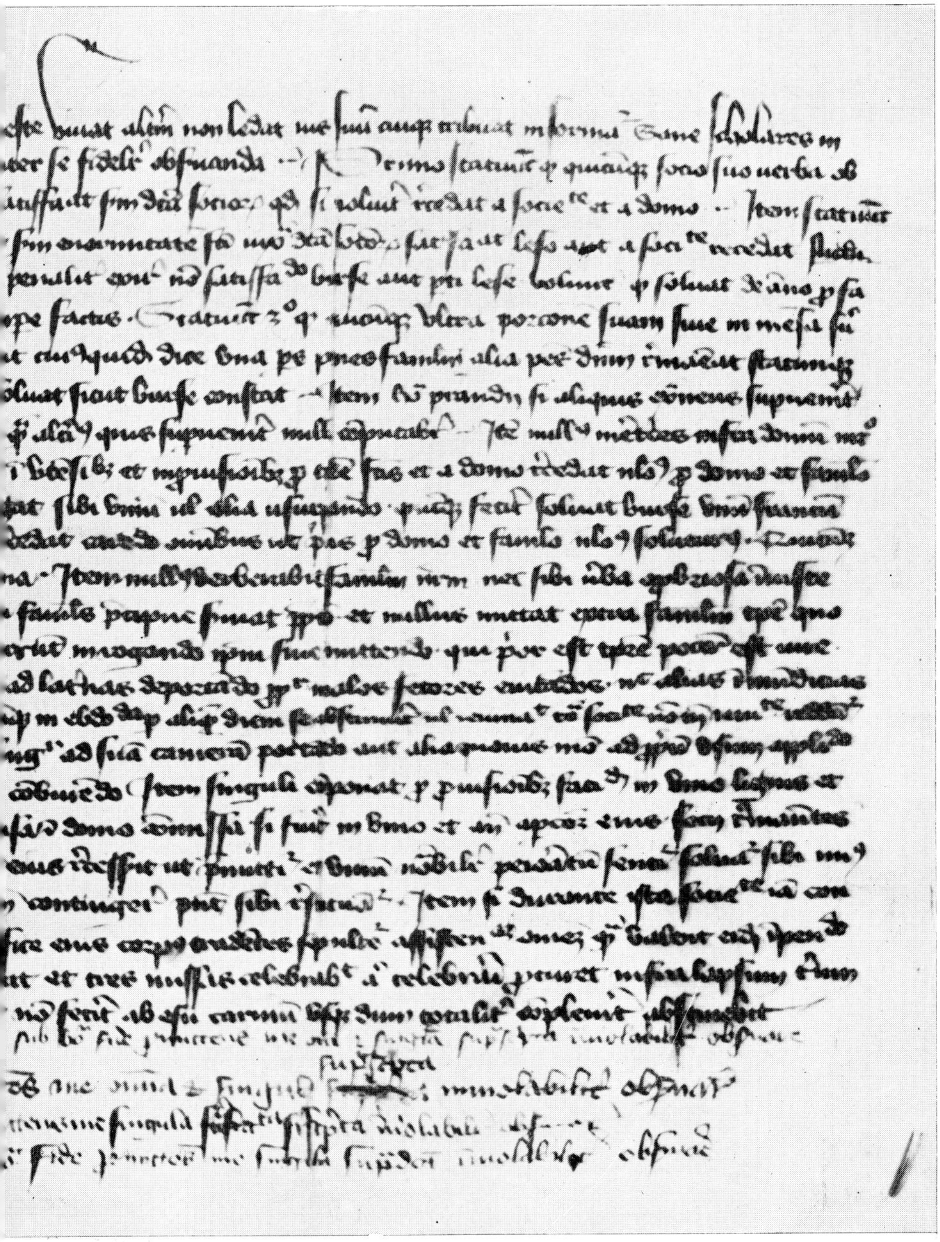

Skara House (ca. 1407).
;go Uddsson (Odonis), procu-
.hop of Skara, 1424-1435).

Paris, *Archives Nationales* M 73. nº 16 [15, XVI].

1) Whoever assails his fellow-scholar with opprobrious or injurious words or with contumely shall pay a *bursa* of one franc and shall satisfy the injured party according to the decision of his associates; if he does not do so, he shall depart from the society and the house.

2) Whoever assaults his fellow-scholar and in fact strikes him [15]), shall pay a *bursa* of two francs and shall satisfy the injured party in accordance with the decision of his fellows, which shall be calculated according to the enormity of the deed; if he does not do so, he shall depart from the society.

3) Whoever wishes to have some wine beyond his portion, whether at mealtime or otherwise, may take it, but shall account for it to the society according to his conscience.

4) Whoever accepts money from the *bursa* to entertain his guests shall pay it back.

5) If an outsider comes at mealtime and eats in the house, the fellow who invited him shall pay for it.

6) No one shall bring prostitutes into the house. If anyone does, he shall pay one franc and shall lose all rights which he had or has to the utensils and provisions and shall depart from the house. Nevertheless, he shall pay the yearly amount for the servant and the rent of the house.

7) No one shall violently break down the gate or the doors of the house in order to take wine or anything else; whoever does this shall pay a *bursa* of one franc and shall repair or have repaired whatever is broken and shall restore whatever is taken. Whoever does not wish to do so shall depart and shall be deprived of all rights as above mentioned. However, he

---

15) Cf. H. BECKMANN, ed., *Johannes Kerer, Statuta Collegii Sapientiae. The Statutes of the Collegium Sapientiae in Freiburg University, Freiburg, Breisgau, 1497*, Lindau & Konstanz, 1957, p. 53.

94

shall still have to pay for room and servant for one year. And whoever breaks glassware, whether accidentally or voluntarily, shall replace it with glassware of better or at least of equal quality.

8) No one shall strike our servant or assail him unjustly with opprobrious words. Whoever does so shall make amends to him and pay a fine according to the decision of the fellows. The servant is to serve first of all the superior of the house. No one may send him on an errand during the time he is to prepare the meals, unless another attends to the servant's chores during his absence. If several members decide to send the servant on an errand at the same period of time, whoever asks first has the priority.

9) Everyone should pay attention to the cleanliness of the house.

10) Whoever is absent or fasting on any day of the week the other members of the house are not fasting shall receive his money back for that day.

11) No one shall take the firewood to his room or apply it in any other way to his own personal use; but rather it shall remain for the common benefit of all, i. e., for preparing meals or for a fire in the *aula* when all are present and agree.

12) Everyone shall share in the cost of the provisions such as wine, wood, and other necessities. And if it happens that someone leaves before the complete consumption of the provisions, not because of some offence committed in the house, he shall be reimbursed in money by the remaining members for his portion of the wine if it has not been opened. If it has been opened, and is found to have deteriorated [16], he shall be paid less according to the judgment of two men experienced in such matters. The rest of the provisions and utensils belonging to him shall be returned to him prior to his departure.

---

16) « et vinum notabiliter pejoratum sentitur » : *Auct.* II, Intr. p. xii; Chart. XVI, 62-63.

13) If God should call one of the fellows from this life, the fellows shall aid the departed honorably by carrying the body
to the grave and by offering every other assistance which is
due him. Moreover, each member shall say his vigil of the
dead and the penitential psalms three times for the repose of
his soul, and shall celebrate three Masses or have three Masses
celebrated within three weeks. Whoever does not do this within
three weeks shall abstain from meat until such time as he
complies.

★

Siggo Uddsson must have left Paris soon after the promulgation
of the Statutes. On April 1, 1410, he was probably already in
Sweden [17]). After his departure Skara House fell into the same
lamentable condition that it was in before. On July 1, 1410, the
Nation complained that the house was again in ruins [18]).

After his return to Sweden, Siggo's career advanced rapidly.
In 1417-18 he participated in the council of Constance [19]). From
August 4, 1418, until his election as bishop of Skara (June 5, 1424),
he was very active as archdeacon [20]).

On his episcopal seal, of 1434 (Plate XXVI), he is shown in a
Gothic setting, kneeling before a crowned Madonna holding the
Divine Child. The architectural decoration around the figures is
supported by his coat of arms [21]). If my deciphering is correct, the

---

17) A deed of the Cathedral Chapter of Linköping, dating from the end of 1410, refers
to Siggo Uddsson as a student of Canon Law in Paris. He was appointed proctor of
Linköping House by the Chapter. The *Liber procuratorum* is silent about his presence
in Paris at that time, and we do not find any reference to his activities as proctor :
Schück, *op. cit.*, p. 68; *D. S. n. s.* II, p. 275, n° 1277; cf. Y. Brilioth, *op. cit.*,
pp. 526; 329; etc., p. 806.

18) *Auct.* II, 78, 38.

19) *D. S. n. s.* III, p. 253, n° 2382. On May 2, 1418, he borrowed 30 « nobulos
[nobiles] anglicanos » in Constance, until he should get to Lübeck : *ibid.*, III, 321,
n° 2469. Å. Sällström, « Nordiska delegater till Konstanz », *Technica et Humaniora*
(1951), 108-109.

20) August 4, 1418 : *ibid.*, III, 354, n° 2512; November 7, 1419 : *ibid.*, p. 517,
n° 2703; February 2, 1420 : *ibid.*, p. 540, n° 2732; cf. L. M. Bååth, ed., *Diplomatarium
Svecanum. Appendix. Acta Pontificum Svecica, I. Acta Cameralia. Vol. II. Ann. 1371-
1492*, Holmiae. 1957, pp. 237, n° 1044; 270, n° 1093; 272, n° 1096.

21) Riksarkivet, Perg. Deed of July 2, 1434.

PLATE XXVI

Seal of Siggo Uddsson, bishop of Skara,
author of the Statutes of Skara House (1434).

Riksarkivet. Perg.

PLATE XXVII

Seal of Karl Uddsson, dean of Skara,
brother of Siggo Uddsson (1412).

D. S. n. s. nº 1626.

legend of this 44 mm. round seal reads : SECRETVM SIGGOIS
DEI GRATIA EPI SCARESIS. The seal of his brother, Karl
Uddsson, priest and dean of Skara, dating from 1412 (Plate XXVII),
bears the same elaborate family arms [22] as Siggo Uddsson's episcopal seal.

After 1425 few students went to Paris from Sweden. Among
the students from the northern part of Europe the majority between
1425 and 1493 came from Åbo [23]. During these years Denmark
was represented at the University of Paris by the dioceses of Odense,
Ribe, and Roskilde [24].

Swedish students came from the dioceses of Vesterås *(Arosiensis)*, Upsala, and Skara. Vesterås sent one student, 1447-1448 [25].
Upsala students were distributed between the years 1436-1437,

---

22) Round, 30 mm., with legend : .S. KAROLI. UDDONIS. PRESBYTERI.
D. S. n. s. II, p. 556, n⁰ 1626 : Deed of September 21, 1412. — The reading in *D. S. n. s.*
is incorrect; instead of KANUTI read KAROLI, to which clear reference is made in
the text : *Karl Udsons.*

23) 15 bachelors (14 became *licentiati* and *incipientes*). Students from Åbo were
registered between 1425-1428; 1431-1433; 1448-1449; 1450-1451; 1461-1462; 1468-1474;
1484-1498 (my statistics are based upon the *Liber receptorum*, H. 2587-2588); cf.
H. HOLMA et A. MALINIEMI, *Les étudiants finlandais à Paris au moyen âge*, Helsinki,
1937. [The dates given below are the years when the students first received a degree
at the University, not when the students first entered Paris.] Andreas Laurentii, alias
Monachi, 1449 (*Auct.* II, 758, 3); Arvidus Corke, later Bishop of Åbo, 1486 (*Auct.* III,
597, 6); Arvidus Jacobi, 1449 (*Auct.* II, 758, 7); Benedictus Olavi, 1427 (*Auct.* II, 358,
33); Conradus Henrici, 1426 (*Auct.* II, 340, 38); Conradus Suart, 1473 (*Auct.* III, 225,
8); Godscalcus Witte, 1460 (*Auct.* II, 928, 29); Gregorius Haffnerlande, 1427 (*Auct.* II,
358, 31); Haquinus Andree, seu Frille, 1461 (*Auct.* II, 934, 24); Henricus Frees, 1451
(*Auct.* II, 850, 32); Henricus Kanuti, 1469 (*Auct.* III, 106, 36); Henricus Nicolai, 1427
(*Auct.* II, 358, 29); Henricus Nicolai de Svecia, 1490 (*Auct.* III, 732, 13); Jacobus
Petri de Roda, 1419 (*Auct.* II, 262, 14), 1425 (*Auct.* II, 337, 14); Johannes Danielis,
1462 (*Auct.* II, 943, 31); Johannes Flicke, 1420 (*Auct.* II, 272, 21); Johannes Magni,
1432 (*Auct.* II, 461, 42); Johannes Olavi de Svecia, later bishop of Åbo, 1485 (*Auct.*
III, 569, n. 5); Johannes Pauli, 1453 (*Auct.* II, 899, 18); Johannes Petri, 1461 (*Auct.* II,
932, 37); Laurentius Hartikim, 1489 (*Auct.* III, 693, 7); Laurentius Michaelis Suurpae,
later bishop of Åbo, 1473 (*Auct.* III, 225, 6, n⁰ 2); Laurentius Rannaldi, 1488 (*Auct.*
III, 663, 12); Magnus Nicolai Särkiläx, later bishop of Åbo, 1456 (*Auct.* II, 910, 39);
Olavus Magni, later bishop of Åbo, 1427 (*Auct.* II, 358, 27, n. 2); Olavus Petri, 1461
(*Auct.* II, 935, 1); Paulus Linguonis, 1489 (*Auct.* III, 643, 3); Petrus Marci, 1449
(*Auct.* II, 763, 38); Severinus Holt, 1427 (*Auct.* II, 358, 25).

24) One student came from Odense, 1446-1447; one from Ribe, 1465-1467; Roskilde
sent three bachelors (3 *licentiati*) who were in Paris during the years 1445-1447,
1467-1468, and 1469-1471.

25) Johannes Langh de Arusia (*Auct.* II, 706, 28).

1459-1460, and 1476-1477, a total of three bachelors mentioned later on as *licentiati* and *incipientes* [26]).

After the return of Siggo Uddsson to Sweden, Skara was represented in Paris by Andreas Arvidi (Arvidsson) in 1440. Andreas received his bachelor's degree that year without any mention of his diocese. He must have left Paris soon afterwards. He died as provost of Skara in 1464 [27]).

It was probably these students from Northern Europe who, during the fifteenth century, inscribed several northern patron saints in the Calendar of the English-German Nation [28]). Feast days of the following patrons of the North are to be found in the Calendar : Saint Olav, King of Norway *(Olavi regis et martyris, regni Norvegie)*, July 29 [29]) ; Saint Eric, King of Sweden and Gotland *(Erici regis et martyris, Suevorum Gothorumque rex)*, May 18 [30]) ; Saint Kanute, King of Denmark *(Passio sancti Kanuti, regis Danie)*, January 7 [31]) ; Saint Henry, bishop of Upsala, made a martyr in 1511 *(Passio sancti Henrici episcopi)*, January 20 [32]), and June 18 : *Translatio sancti Henrici episcopi et martyris, patroni Aboensium gloriosi* [33]).

---

26) Ingolphus Olavi, 1477 (*Auct.* III, 348, 31) ; Jacobus Ulfonis, 1460 (*Auct.* II, 927, 20) ; Laurentius Olavi de Thuna, 1436 (*Auct.* II, 491, 27) ; Petrus Johannis Galle, 1477 (*Auct.* III, 347, 36).

27) In 1440 he was immatriculated into the University of Cologne. H. KEUSSEN, *Die Matrikel der Universität Köln 1389-1475*, Bonn, 1928, I, p. 431. He went to Perugia in 1449, and died as provost of Skara (G. CARLSSON, « Paris-Uppsala. Ett stycke tidig svensk universitetshistoria », *Kyrkohistorisk Årsskrift* 55 [1955] 233) : K. H. KARLSSON, « Electus Björn i Skara samt Striderna om domprosteriet i Skara 1449-1475 », *Kyrkohistorisk Årsskrift* 6 (1905), 29; *Auct.* II, 511, 32.

28) Paris, B. N. N. a. lat. 535. Cf. E. CHATELAIN, « Le „ Livre ” ou „ Cartulaire ” de la Nation d'Angleterre et d'Allemagne dans l'ancienne université de Paris », *Mémoires de la Société de l'Histoire de Paris* 18 (1891), 73-100; H. OMONT, « Nouvelles acquisitions du Département des Manuscrits de la Bibliothèque Nationale », *Bibliothèque de l'École des Chartes*, 53 (1892), 340.

29) B. N. N. a. lat. 535, fol. 10 recto.

30) *Ibid.*, fol. 9 recto.

31) *Ibid.*, fol. 7 recto; cf. also the so-called « Calendar of Peter of Dacia » ca. 1290 : Jan. 7, *Kanuti ducis*; July 10, *Kanuti regis*; J. LANGEBEK - P. F. SUHM, *Scriptores rerum Danicarum Medii Aevi*, Hauniae, Tom. VI, pp. 261-263.

32) GEIJER - SCHRÖDER, *Scriptores rerum Svecicarum*, II, 331-343.

33) B. N. N. a. lat. 535, fol. 9 verso; P. PERDRIZET, *Le Calendrier de la Nation d'Allemagne de l'ancienne Université de Paris* (Publications de la Faculté des Lettres de l'Université de Strasbourg, nᵒ 79), Paris, 1937, pp. 51-54.

XII

SKARA HOUSE,
AN UNDISPUTED PROPERTY
OF THE NATION

In 1442, thirty years after the departure of Siggo, the last legitimate tenant, the English-German Nation was still fully aware that Skara House belonged neither to the Nation nor to the Province of Sweden but to the Church of Skara [1]). In the absence of students from Sweden, Boemundus the beadle still lived in the southern part of the house, Jacobus Winthorst de Hamburg [2]) in the northern, or lower part.

After the death of Boemundus, in 1453 [3]), the government of the House automatically returned to the Nation. Since, to be rented profitably, the house had to be repaired, the proctor, his deputies, and repairmen visited it in 1456 [4]). In their report they distin-

---

1) « Que nec est pro natione nec pro provincia, sed pro ecclesia Scarensi » : *Auct.* II, 534, 17.

2) Jacobus Winthorst of Hamborch (Hamburg) de Saxonia, from the dioc. of Bremen : *Auct.* II, 507, 2; bachelor at Rostock in 1435 : A. HOFMEISTER, *Die Matrikel der Universität Rostock*, Rostock, 1889, I, 54; intitulatus in Cologne 1436 : KEUSSEN, *Matrikel Köln*, I, 391; received among the bachelors at Paris in 1437 : *Auct.* II, 501, 23. Left Paris soon because of the plague ravaging the city. Returned in 1438 when we find him among the *hospites* of the College of Sorbonne : B. N. ms. Lat. 16070, p. 61; Arsenal 1228, fol. 348 recto. Receptor of the English-German Nation in 1439, 1441 : *Auct.* II, 998. Proctor in 1441, 1442, 1444. *Ibid.*, II, 992, 993. Bachelor of Sacred Theology in 1444 : *ibid.*, II, 582, 25. No mention of him is to be found after 1444, March 24 : *Auct.* II, 585, 27. Cf. Arch. Nat. H. 2587, fol. 25 recto.

3) *Auct.* II, 902, 4.

4) *Liber receptorum*, Arch. Nat. H 2587, fol. 105 recto : the roofer received 8 alb., the proctor and deputies 10 alb.

guished carefully between « the house with the sign of Notre-Dame » and another house that had no distinctive sign. The repairs of the latter came to 32 sol. [5]). After the renovation they rented it to a certain Vrou Sandikens [6]).

The Nation consulted, for some unknown reasons, the title deeds of Skara House in 1464 [7]); additional repairs were needed in the following years, 1466 [8]), 1469 [9]), but the work must have been carried out rather hastily, because in 1476 one of the houses was again in lamentable condition. By now, beadle Goswinus Schopenhagel [Schuppenaghel, Schopenagel] [10]), successor of Boemundus, rented the house [11]) together with the house of Saint-Michel [12]), which had been bequeathed to the Nation by Boemundus, and spent more than 50 francs for renovations. Skara House was again given to the beadle of the Nation for his lifetime, for 2 francs yearly [13]),

---

5) *Ibid.*, cf. M 73, n° 5 [V]; M 73, n° 7 [VII].

6) During the 1456-1457 schoolyear she paid 21 sol. until October 1 for one term (H 2587, fol. 109 recto); 1 scutum to Christmas *(ibid.)*; 1 scutum 13 sol. for the rest of the year *(ibid.*, fol. 112 recto).

7) H 2587, fol. 18 recto : 2 sol. fee was given to the consultant.

8) *Auct.* III, 5, 5. The expression « domorum ecclesie Scarensis » refers to the house called Notre-Dame and that « without a sign » : *Auct.* III, 8, 2.

9) *Ibid.*, III, 103, 44 - 104, 5.

10) Goswinus Schuppennagel is mentioned as a minor beadle in 1455 : Arch. Nat. H 2587, fol. 102 recto; he became a major beadle in 1462 : *ibid.*, H 2588, fol. 2 recto. On September 24, 1489, he gave a *cedula* to the English-German Nation concerning the three houses he rented from the Nation, among them Skara House : Arch. Nat. M 73; in 1499 he was still a major beadle : Sorbonne, Reg. 91, fol. 30 recto.

11) The proctor speaks of three houses : « suis tribus domibus quas a natione habuit ad vitam » : *Auct.* III, 713, 29. These three houses were the house with the sign Notre-Dame, another « without a sign » (these two formed Skara House), and the house of Saint-Michel. Cf. *Auct.* III, 319, 18 : « Quarumdam domorum pertinencium ecclesie Scarensi in Suecia ».

12) The house of Saint-Michel had been acquired by Boemundus on July 12, 1415, from Oliverius de Imperio [Olivier de l'Empire] (*Chart. Univ. Paris.* IV, p. 299, n° 2042). According to the contract of sale dated on the day after the purchase (M 73 [Liasse C] n° 19), this house was located between the house of Chastel and another house of Boemundus. After the death of Boemundus the Nation took it over. In a deed of June 17, 1461, (M 73, n° 21) its location is described as « tenant d'une part à Pierre Hagues et d'autre part aux escolles de decret ou est pour enseigne l'imaige Saint-Eustace. » In the seventeenth century it is sometimes referred to as « Maison du Double-Aigle » (Arch. Nat. M 73 n°ˢ 18-24).

13) *Auct.* III, 319, 17-37. In 1479 Goswinus paid 16 sol. for a half year « pro domo Scarensi » : H 2588, fol. 77 recto.

and he was reminded that the houses must be in good order when they were returned [14].

On September 24, 1481, Goswinus referred to certain title deeds « obtained from the founders » that allegedly freed him from the obligation of paying rent, but the Nation, indignantly accusing him of fraudulent interpretation of the agreement, ordered the beadle to fulfill his obligations [15]. On September 19, 1489, the Nation requested of Goswinus a formal agreement concerning the lease of the houses [16]. The result of the energetic demand of the Nation is the receipt dated September 22, 1489, which we possess today among the title deeds of Skara House. In this receipt the property of the canons of Skara is identified as « une maison contenant deux corps d'ostel... au dessus des escolles de decrett en l'une desquelles est pour enseigne l'*Image Nostre Dame* » [17].

As I have mentioned at the beginning of Chapter I, one of the main reasons why the title deeds of Skara House were kept together was that the Nation needed them many times to back up its claim to the houses. On January 13, 1486, the Nation was summoned to the Châtelet as defendant against the canons of Saint-Benoît-Bien-Tourné, who claimed certain rents on Skara House [18]. The Nation, despite the fact that three masters consulted the title deeds [19], must have been sentenced to pay the canons what was due, because on April 27, 1486, Petrus Caesaris [Wagner] [20], receptor, paid 12 sol. paris. to Robert de Sauchoy, proctor and receptor of the said canons : « pour raison et à cause d'une maison seant en la Rue du Cloz Bruneau nommé l'ostel de Suesse où quel est l'*Ymaige Notre Dame* » [21]. The Nation from now on fulfilled its financial

---

14) *Auct.* III, 319, 33.

15) *Ibid.*, III, 482, 20-30.

16) *Ibid.*, III, 713, 28, 40.

17) Arch. Nat. M 73, Liasse E.

18) *Auct.* III, 595, 45 - 596, 2.

19) « Regestra similiter et cartas dicte domus » : *Auct.* III, 596, 24.

20) He was from Silesia, dioc. of Posen. Master of Arts in 1463 (*Auct.* II, 948, 20, where *licentiatus*) ; proctor 1466, 1468, 1490 (*ibid.*, III, 825, 830) ; receptor 1469, 1479, 1484, 1485 (*ibid.*, 831-32), and 1503 (Sorb. Reg. 91 [85], fol. 56 verso) ; 1474-1478 with John Stoll at « Chevalier au Cygne » : A. CLAUDIN, *Liste chronologique des imprimeurs parisiens du quinzième siècle, 1470-1500*, Paris, 1901, p. 8. Died 1509 : F. STOCK, *Die ersten deutschen Buchdrucker in Paris um 1500* (Volksdeutsche Quellen und Darstellungen no 1) Freiburg in Br., 1940, p. 83.

21) M 73, no 17 [16, XVII].

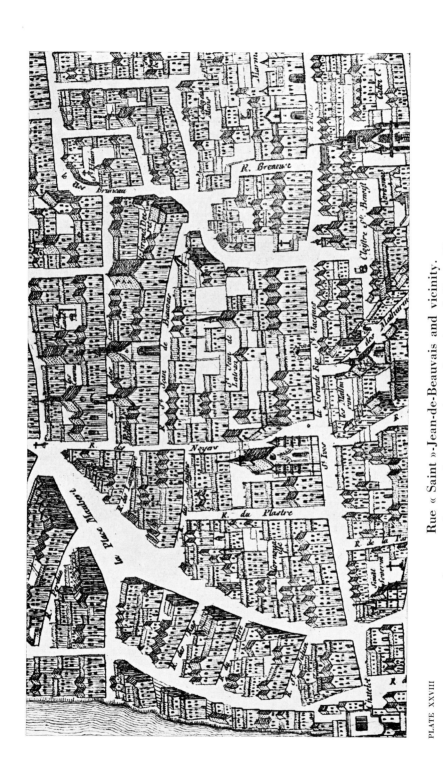

PLATE XXVIII

Rue « Saint » Jean-de-Beauvais and vicinity.
Arrow points to the approximate location of Skara House.

Map of Dheulland [1756].
Paris sous le Règne de Charles IX.
New York Public Library Collection.

obligations more faithfully and made payments to the canons for Skara House as late as December 31, 1502 [22]).

There is no record or at least no explicit mention of any students from the diocese of Skara around 1489. However the English-German Nation granted the request of a certain Nicholaus Vos, native of Gand, to serve as messenger *(nuntius)* in behalf of the masters and students from the diocese of Skara. It is possible that Nicholaus Vos had some private business in Skara and that he simply wanted to be authorized by the Nation to act as messenger should some business arise between the diocese of Skara and the University of Paris [23]).

Between 1501 and 1503 the houses of the Nation needed new repairs. In 1503, during the receptorship of Petrus Caesaris, 7 lib. 8 den. were paid out for the house of Notre-Dame [24]). Thereafter Skara House, one part of it from now on called *Notre-Dame* or *Image de Notre-Dame,* became one of the most prosperous real estate possessions of the Nation [25]). It was rented many times to various tenants until the first part of the eighteenth century, so far as we can establish from the records at our disposal in the collection M 73 [26]), seemingly more often than any of the other houses of the Nation located in Rue « Saint »-Jean-de-Beauvais, in the vicinity of the Grandes-Ecoles-de-Droit and the College of Beauvais.

---

22) In 1493 it paid 14 sol. par. « pro canonicis Sancti-Benedicti pro fundo terre domus Scharensis » : H 2588, fol. 135 recto; in 1502, 13 sol. 11 den. obul. paris. : M 73, n° 17 [XVIII]; cf. the note in the *Liber receptorum,* Sorbonne, Arch. Reg. 91 (85) fol. 54 recto : « Item dedi domino procuratori Licorne de Sancto-Benedicto de quinque annis de domo nostra sita in vico Brunelli per manus magistri Petrus Cesaris... 13 sol. paris. 11 den. paris. »

23) *Auct.* III, 716, 33.

24) Sorbonne, Arch. Reg. 91 (85) fol. 59 verso : « Item pro reparacionibus factis de domo nacionis vbi est signum Nostre Domine vij lib. viij den. paris. » Cf. *ibid.,* fol. 39 verso and 41 verso : « in domo Gossuini super materia domorum. »

25) In 1501 the English-German Nation possessed three houses. The first, called *magna domus,* was leased to a troublesome woman *(pessima mulier),* says the receptor. Her rents could be collected only with great difficulty *(magno labore* [Sorbonne, Arch. Reg. 91 (85) fol. 49 recto]). The second house was rented to Goswinus, minor beadle; the third, to Philippus, provost *(ibid.,* fol. 39 verso).

26) Leases : 1544, May to Barthelemy Morel, official of the Archdeacon of Paris; 1578, August 26; 1635, March 20; 1677, July 15; 1703, October 20; 1719, August 1; 1729, March 28; 1735, May 7; 1737, September 15 : Arch. Nat. M 73, n°s 31-40.

PART II

TOPOGRAPHY OF SKARA HOUSE

TOPOGRAPHY

OF SKARA HOUSE

The first description of the location of the house which was to become Skara House occurs in a deed of January 13, 1284, when it was still owned by beadle Guillelmus Biterne [1]). It was situated in Clos-Bruneau [2]), in Paris, on the Left Bank of the Seine. The southern side of the house was adjacent to the houses of Radulphus Scriptor and Nicolaus *Taillator pannorum*. On the other side it was adjacent to another building, also owned by Guillelmus Biterne [3]).

Very precious information about the position of Skara House is given in the letter of sale dated September 10, 1292. Here the house was described as two units *(duas domos)* [4]) which later on were identified as « adjacent to each other » *(sibi ad inuicem attinenti-*

---

1) M 73, nᵒ 1 [I].

2) « Ultra Paruum Pontem in clauso Brunelli » *(ibid.)*. The *Clos-Bruneau, Brunelli, Burnel*, many times spelled *Burnelli*, was named after a *clos* or vineyard that belonged to the Chapter of Saint-Marcel. It was bounded by Rue des-Noyers, Rue des-Carmes, Rue « Saint »-Jean-de-Beauvais, and Rue du-Clos-Bruneau *(vicus Brunelli* or *Burnelli)* : H. SAUVAL, *Histoire et recherches des antiquités de la ville de Paris*, Paris, 1733, II, 360 [Livre VIII]; H. GÉRAUD, *Paris sous Philippe le Bel, d'après des documents originaux et notamment d'après un manuscrit contenant le rôle de la taille imposée sur les habitants de Paris en 1292*, Paris, 1837, pp. 330-331; [J. B.] JAILLOT, *Recherches critiques, historiques et topographiques sur la ville de Paris, depuis ses commencements connus jusqu'à présent*, Paris, 1782, IV. (Quartier Saint-Benoît) p. 167; J. LEBEUF, *Histoire de la ville et de tout le diocèse de Paris*, Paris, 1883, I, 354, note 13; cf. K. MICHAËLSSON, *Le livre de la taille de Paris l'an 1296* (Romanica Gothoburgensia nᵒ 7), Göteborg, 1958, p. 247, note 3.

3) « Et ex altera [parte] cuidam alteri domui ipsorum Guillermi et eius vxoris » : M 73, nᵒ 2 [II]; cf. also « et ex alio latere cuidam alii domui ipsorum coniugum » : M 73, nᵒ 5 [V]; cf. M 73, nᵒ 1 [I].

4) M 73, nᵒ 5 [V].

bus) [5]) and as « two houses, looking almost as one » *(duas domos que pro una reputantur)* [6]). This description is very precious, for without it we could not understand the fifteenth and sixteenth-century partition of Skara House into two separate houses, first into one that had « no sign » and another with the sign *Image de Notre-Dame* [7]), and in the sixteenth century into the *Maison du Cadran* and the *Maison de Notre Dame* [8]).

In 1292, when Emphastus, canon of Växjö, bought the house (I shall use the singular for the two houses that formed one building), it was bordered on the south by the houses of Guillelmus Calot Burgundus and the late Robertus Blondi and on the north by the properties of Guillelmus Orvalle and his wife, heirs of Guillelmus Biterne [9]). From behind, it was adjacent to the houses of Matheus de Orto Lombardi and of Petrus de Villa Blovana. The back part of the property extended to a dead-end street *(ruella sine capite)*, Rue Josselin [10]), or *ruella Jocelini Anglici* [11]). In 1299 the southern neighbor was still Guillelmus Calot Burgundus. The wall between his house and that of Emphastus belonged to both of them [12]).

The small house or *masura* bought by Emphastus in 1300 was located in Rue Josselin and was opposite a certain house called La Palmière [13]). The *masura* bordered the house belonging

---

5) M 73, n⁰ 7 [VII] : February 4, 1293; M 73, n⁰ 5 [V] : September 10, 1292; M 73, n⁰ 8 [VIII] : July 19, 1298 : « ad inuicem attinentes ».

6) M 73, n⁰ 8 [VIII] : July 19, 1298.

7) *Liber receptorum*, H 2587, fol. 105 verso [1456] : « Item pro reformacione domus scarensis in qua non est intersignium... xxxij sol. »; cf. also « *de ymaginis nostre Domine* » [1392] *Auct.* I, 661, 35; *Auct.* II, 912, 27.

8) On the back of the deed of February 6, 1285 (M 73, n⁰ 2 [II]), there is a note in an eighteenth-century hand : « Ces maisons sont celles du Quadran et de Notre Dame, anciennement appellée Domus Scarensis ou Hostel de Swecie. La maison de St. Michel ne fut acquise qu'en l'an 1415. »

9) M 73, n⁰ 5 [V].

10) Jaillot thought that rue Josselin did not exist in the thirteenth century : *Recherches* IV (Quartier Saint-Benoît), 105-6. Our document clearly shows that the *allée* existed as early as September 10, 1292. Originally rue Josselin was a road through Clos-Bruneau. Later it was called *cul-de-sac-Bouvard* : LEBEUF, *op. cit.*, I, 129; 354, note 13; cf. M 73 n⁰ 11 [X].

11) M 73, n⁰ 10 [XI] : February 3, 1309.

12) M 73, n⁰ 9 [IX].

13) M 73, n⁰ 11 [X]. I wonder if this *masura* is the *stabulum* mentioned in 1405 as belonging to the Swedish students : « De domo *ad ymaginem nostre Domine...*

to the Mathurins [14]) on one side and Skara House itself on the other side.

On February 3, 1309, a new owner, beadle Briffaut, lived next to Skara House, probably on the northeast side. His property reached on one side the house of Pierre Felisc and on the other side Skara House, which is identified here as « maeson qui est aus clers escoliers d'Alemaigne » [15]).

No special name was given to Skara House in the 1385 livery of seisin obtained by Brynulphus Karlsson [16]). A few years later, in 1392, one of the two adjacent houses forming the Skara building was identified for the first time as *de ymaginis nostre Domine* [17]). The southern or upper part, « towards Sainte-Geneviève », was given to beadle Boemundus, while the other, the northern or lower part, « towards the College of Beauvais » [18]), was put up for rent. The two houses still formed a unit, and in 1442 they were described as *domus iste due sub eodem tecto* [19]).

In 1466 Skara House is mentioned as being located above the *Scolae Decretorum* [20]), therefore south of it, because Montagne-Sainte-Geneviève rises to the south. The building of the *Grand Décret* (Ecoles de Droit, Col. de Droit Canon) is usually well marked on the old maps of Paris. It was located between the College of

---

Bumundus... haberet medietatem ejusdem domus, que pars est versus Sanctam Geno-wefam cum medietate cavee et orto, qui est retro, eciam *cum stabulo* » (*Auct.* I, 908, 40).

14) Or Trinitarians. The house previously belonged to frater Jacobus de Duaco, *ordinis Sancti Mathurini* (M 73, n° 9 [IX]), a Mathurin. The Mathurins may have inherited this house from Master Robertus Blondi, who owned it before 1292 (M 73, n° 5 [V]). His anniversary was inscribed into the obituary of the Mathurins in Paris on June 2 : A. MOLINIER, *Obituaires de la province de Sens* (Recueil des Historiens de la France. Obituaires) Paris, 1902, I, 2, p. 687.

15) M 73, n° 14 [13, XIV].

16) M 73, n° 15 [14, XV].

17) *Auct.* I, 661, 35.

18) « Que pars est versus Sanctam Genowefam » : *Auct.* I, 908, 38; *D. S.* IV, 181-82, n° 3060; the northern or lower part « que respicit collegium Belvacense » : *Auct.* I, 909, 20.

19) *Auct.* II, 534, 17, 22.

20) « Primus articulus super dispositione domorum ecclesie Scarensis que situate sunt in vico Clausi Brunelli supra scolas Decretorum » : *Auct.* III, 4, 34. Cf. deed of September 22, 1489 (M 73, Liasse E) : « au dessus des escolles de decrett »; cf. chapter XII, note 17; J. DU BREUL, *Le Théatre des antiquitez de Paris*, Paris, 1612, pp. 749-751.

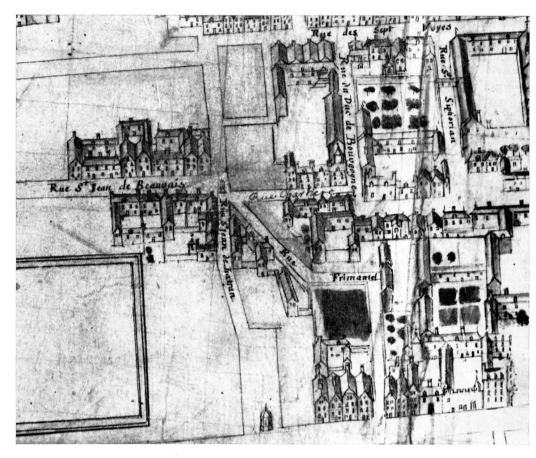

Rue des Sept Voyes
Rue St Sulpician
Rue du Duc de Bourgogne
Rue St Jean de Beauvais
Clos Charlier
Rue St Jean de Latran
Frimault

PLATE XXIX

Rue « Saint »-Jean-de-Beauvais and its neighborhood
in the censive of Sainte-Geneviève.

Arch. Nat. N. II. 32.
Seigneurie et censive de l'abbaye Sainte-Geneviève...
Vue cavalière. Ech. 1/600 [i.e. the original].

Beauvais and Rue Saint-Hilaire (sometimes called Rue Fromentel, or Puits-Certain) [21]). The general location of Skara House was, therefore, between the *Grand Décret* and Rue Saint-Hilaire in Rue « Saint »-Jean-de-Beauvais, on the east side of the street. (Plate XXVIII)

Next to Skara House was a building that belonged to Boemundus before he bought the house of Saint-Michel. After his death these two houses were taken over by the Nation. The first, adjacent to Skara House, was later called *Parvae Scholae Decretales* (Petites-Ecoles-de-Décret) [22]). Next to it was the house of Saint-Michel [23]). The southern location of the latter is shown by a statement of the proctor in 1466 : *domus in intersignio sancti Michaelis que est supra domus ecclesie Scarensis situata* [24]).

The order of houses from the *Grand Décret* to the south was as follows : Skara House (Notre-Dame and the other house « without a sign »), the *Parvae Scholae Decretales*, and the house of Saint-Michel.

The chartulary of the English-German Nation carefully listed, on December 9, 1500, the conditions governing the leasing of the three houses belonging to the Nation, in order that all the masters, young and old, should know how and under what circumstances these houses were to be rented. The Nation stipulated that this list

---

21) A. Franklin, *Les anciens plans de Paris. Notices historiques et topographiques*, Paris, 1878, I, 22, 48, 65. *Plan en Perspective de la ville de Paris telle qu'elle était sous le Règne de Charles IX. Gravé d'après une Tapisserie conservée dans l'Hôtel de Ville*. Dheulland delin., 1756 [Plate XXVIII]. See L. Vallée, *Catalogue des plans de Paris et des cartes*, Paris, 1908, p. 420, n° 3440; *Plan détaillé du Quartier de Ste-Geneviève. Levé géométriquement par Feu M. l'abbé de La Grive Géographe de la ville de Paris... Fini et Publié par Al. Fr. Hugnin*, Paris, 1757 [Plate XXX]. Cf. L. Vallée, *op. cit.*, p. 199, n° 1530.

22) « Nota que dans le corps de ce contract [that of the house of Saint-Michel] il est dit que cette maison de S. Michel tient d'un côté à l'Hotel du Chatel (c'est à présent la maison du Sr. Ballard) et de l'autre à celle dudit Boemond de Luttre, Bedel de Nation d'Angleterre. C'est la maison qui fut appelée dans la suite *Les petites Ecoles de Décret* » : Sorbonne, Arch. Carton 14, Liasse 3, n° 37, p. 5. In 1501 the receptor remarked that this house also belonged at one time to the Nation : « Item ad reparandum coopertorium tecti magne domus nostre in vico Brunelli site prope paruas scholas decretorum que (ut dicitur) etiam quondam ad nationem nostram spectabant... 2 lib. 12 sol. » : Sorbonne, Arch. Reg. 91 (85) fol. 42 recto.

23) See the preceding note and cf. chapter XII, note 12.

24) *Auct.* III, 5, 17. *Supra* indicates southern location, because Montagne-Sainte-Geneviève rises to the south.

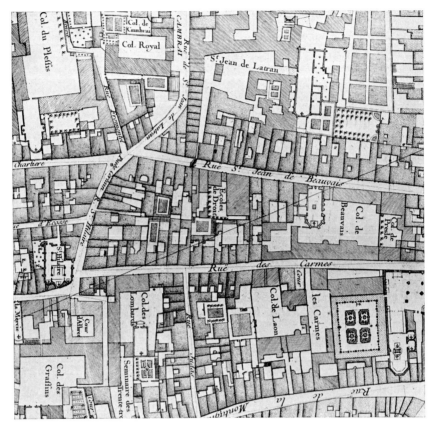

PLATE XXX

Rue « Saint »-Jean-de-Beauvais.
Arrow points to the approximate location of Skara House.

Map of Al. Fr. Hugnin [1757].
Plan levé par l'abbé de La Grive.
Charles Liebman Collection, New York City.

of conditions should be read whenever the receptor of the Nation gave his accounts *(computus)* [25]).

The first house belonging to the Nation, a large stone house *(magna et lapidea)* [26]), was rented for twenty-one francs to « Anthonette, femme de Jehan Hugier ». This was the house of Saint-Michel, identified also as *domus major*, « *Scilicet Imaginis sancti Michaelis* » [27]). It was located in Clos-Bruneau, « rue de Beauvais, » adjoining the *Petites Ecoles de Décret* on one side, and on the other, a house belonging to the heirs of a certain Master Jehan [28]). This *magna domus* was mentioned several times by the receptor of the English-German Nation in the year 1501-1502. It is clear that he was definitely referring to the house of Saint-Michel [29]), and that he had correctly reported that the house was rented to a woman the « French » called Anthonette.

The second house, *domus parva*, was rented for 12 francs to Goswinus, a beadle [30]).

The third house, bearing the sign of Our Lady *(in Intersigno Nostre Domine)*, rented for ten royal *écus* anually [31]). This was the former Skara House, and was rented on September 19, 1500, to « Maistre Crespin prevost, maistre ès ars, licencié en Décret » for three years [32]). It was situated on *rue Cloz Brunel*, flanked by another house belonging to the Nation and by a house belonging to the heirs of Masters Henry Alexandre [33]).

---

25) Paris, B.N. N.a.lat. 535, fol. 153 recto : « Hic sequuntur instrumenta super locatione domorum Venerande Nacionis Alamanie que sepius in anno legi debent ad finem omnes magistri, tam juvenes quam senes, poterunt scire quomodo et quantum locate sunt prefate domus, et quibus; et quomodo in futurum locari debent, et per tempus ut patet in instrumento inferius posito ».

26) *Ibid.*, fol. 154 recto and fol. 153 recto.

27) *Ibid.*, fol. 153 recto.

28) *Ibid.*

29) « Item a muliere manente in magna domo nostra quam mulierem Galli Anthonette nominant » [1501] : Sorbonne, Reg. 91 (85) fol. 37 recto; cf. the repair of the house « magne domus nostre », *ibid.*, fol. 42 recto; see above, note 22.

30) B.N. N.a.lat. 535, fol. 154 recto.

31) *Ibid.*, « Tercia domus que est in Intersigno Nostre Domine est locata pro decem scutis reg. quolibet anno ».

32) *Ibid.*, fol. 153 verso : « Sequitur obligatio magistri Crispini preuoist, licentiati in Decretis, qui locauit domum aliam vbi Ymago Beate Virginis est posita ».

33) *Ibid.* : « ... assise à Paris rue de Cloz Brunel, et tenant aux hoirs feu maistre Henry Alexandre d'une part et d'autre à une autre maison appartenant à la ditte Nation ».

The earliest *censiers* of the Abbey of Sainte-Geneviève do not mention Skara House. Among the later ones, a *censier* of 1497 [34]) refers only to the house of Saint-Michel where the beadle Goswinus lived, owing, at this time, 20 sol. of rent.

A 1543-1544 *censier* of Sainte-Geneviève [35]) makes distinct mention of four houses belonging to the Nation, namely : 1) Saint-Michel, inhabited by « Goussouin bedeau d'Almaigne »; 2) *Petites Ecoles de Décret;* 3) a house identified only as rented to a *patissier* [Jacques Glane] [36]) ; 4) the house of Notre-Dame (once Skara House), the tenant of which was Master Jehan Missart, which adjoined the house of Master Simon Dodier. The Nation paid 20 sol. censes for these houses.

The *censier* of 1547 gives the same descriptions as the previous one, mentioning in addition Jacques Glane, the tenant of the third house [37]). Years later, in a 1581 *censier* [38]), these houses were referred to simply as *quatre corps d'hostel,* owing 20 sol. censes to the Abbey of Sainte-Geneviève. (Plate XXIX)

A. Berty in his *Topographie du vieux Paris* refers to a *censier* (which he does not identify, beyond saying that it was made a few years after 1544) mentioning four houses owned by the Nation, namely : Saint-Michel, *Petites Ecoles de Décret, Maison du Cadran (Quadran),* and *Image de Notre-Dame.* The *Maison du Cadran*

---

34) Arch. Nat. S. 1630⁶ : *Recepte faicte par moy frere Jehan le Maistre pitancier et cuisinier de l'Eglise Madame Saincte-Geneviefue au Mont de Paris* [1497], fol. 38 verso.

35) Arch. Nat. S. 1631⁸ : *Recepte faicte par moy frere Jehan Garsonnet, prestre, religieux et pitancyer de l'Eglise et Abbaye Madame Saincte-Geneviefue au Mont de Paris,* [1544], fol. 58 recto and verso : « La premiere est celle de l'Imaige Sainct Michel devant declarée. La seconde sont les Petittes Escolles de Décret et la baillée aussy à longue année. La tierce est à [blank space] patissier tenant aux dittes Petittes Escolles. La quarte est la maison où demeure Maitre Jehan Missart où est pour enseigne sur la pourte l'Imaige Nostre Dame tenant à la maison ou se tient Maistre Simon Dodier qui est des appartenances des Grandes Escolles de Décret ».

36) Arch. Nat. S. 1632, fol. 67 verso : « La tierce est à Jacques Glane, patissier, tenant ausdittes Petittes Escolles. » Jacques Glane's name was inserted here in another hand.

37) Arch. Nat. S. 1632 : *Recepte faicte par moy, frere Michel de Reilhac, prestre, religieux et pitancyer de l'Eglise et Abbaye Madame Saincte-Geneviefue au Mont de Paris,* [1547], fol. 67 verso and recto; cf. 1548, fol. 85 verso; 1549, fol. 88 verso.

38) Arch. Nat. S. 1633 : *Recepte faicte par moy frere Hector Barreau relligieux et pictancier de l'Eglise et Abbaye Madame Saincte-Geneviefue au Mont de Paris,* [1581], fol. 20 recto : « De la Nation d'Allemaigne qui doibt vingt solz paris. pour leur maison, contenant quatre corps d'Hostel... xx. sol. Paris. » Cf. also [1584], *ibid.,* fol. 39 recto.

was the part of Skara House that had no distinctive sign *(in qua non est intersignium)* [39]. This was confirmed by a seventeenth-century description of the properties of the Nation. According to 1655 and 1678 documents [40], the house of *Notre-Dame* was adjacent to the *Maison du Cadran* [41]. This latter, in turn, was next to the *Parvae Scholae Decretorum*, which was adjacent to the house of *Saint-Michel*, also called *Maison du Double-Aigle* (Plate XXX).

To sum up : Skara House [42] was located on the east side of Rue « Saint »-Jean-de-Beauvais, south of the College of Beauvais, between the *Grand Décret* and Rue Saint-Hilaire.

The approximate location of Skara House would correspond today to the southeast corner of the intersection of Rue des-Ecoles and Rue Jean-de-Beauvais, or, more exactly, with the angle formed by two present houses : n° 43 Rue des-Ecoles and n° 15 Rue Jean-de-Beauvais. The house may have been torn down when the present Rue des-Ecoles was laid down. Thus Skara House was located between the present n° 15 and n° 13 of Rue Jean-de-Beauvais, east of the square in front of the Collège de France, in the heart of the *Quartier Latin*.

---

39) *Auct.* II, 912, 28; BERTY, *Topographie*, VI, p. 100.

40) Two *Mémoires*, dated 1655 and 1678, designate the houses under the following names :
1) Skara House : the building with the sign *Notre Dame;*
2) another : the building with the sign *Cadran;*
3) *Petites Ecoles de Décret :* the building with the sign *Le Murier;*
4) Saint-Michel : the building with the sign *Double-Aigle.* These were the « quatre maisons attenante l'une l'autre » owned by the English-German Nation in the seventeenth century : Arch. Nat., M 73, n° 23 and n° 24. Cf. BERTY, *Topographie*, VI, p. 100.

41) Arch. Nat. M 73, n° 25 [1678] : « Item une autre maison où est pour enseigne le Cadran, tenant d'une part à la maison cy dessus des dites Petites Escolles de Décret, d'autre à la maison suivante... Item une autre maison seize en la mesme rüe Saint-Jean-de-Beauvais où est pour enseigne sur la porte l'Image Nostre-Dame, tenant d'un costé à la precedente, d'autre a la veuve ou ayans cause, Antoine Gallot, vivant, notaire apostolique. »

42) The last description of the houses I have found is dated October 7, 1733 : « Ou pend pour Enseigne l'Image Notre Dame appartenante laditte Nation, consistante en une boutique, salle, cave, séparée en deux par une cloison de planches de batteau; cour derrière cy devans en jardin, deux étages de chambres au dessus desditte boutiques salle et grenier » : Arch. Nat. M 73, n° 56 [p. 2].

CONCLUSION

The hundred and fifty-year history of Skara House (1292-1435) clearly shows that the bishops of Skara were deeply interested in this hospice for Swedish students studying at the University of Paris. Emphastus bought the house in 1292 during the bishopric of Brynulphus Algotsson (1278-1317), who had been a student for many years in Paris. Emphastus remained interested in the House even after his departure from Paris, handling his business through his proctor Sueno, a Swedish scholar studying in Paris. Another Brynulphus, Brynulphus Karlsson, lived in Skara House as its proctor, and remained solicitous for the House during his episcopate (1405-1424). The reformer of discipline and liturgical life in Skara House, Siggo Uddsson, author of the Statutes (around 1407) of the community of scholars living in Skara House, finished his career as bishop of Skara (1424-1435).

Skara House was located on the east side of Rue Clos-Bruneau, which later became Rue « Saint »-Jean-de-Beauvais (today Rue Jean-de-Beauvais). From behind it extended to a dead-end street, Rue Josselin, later on called Bouvard. Towards the end of the fourteenth century its position was more precisely described as being located between the School of Canon Law, called *Grand Décret*, and Rue Saint-Hilaire.

The documents pertaining to the history of Skara House reveal a number of hitherto unknown inhabitants and owners of houses in Clos-Bruneau, from around 1285 to around 1299 : Guillebertus de Volta; Guillelmus Biterne, beadle of the French Nation, and his wife Johanna; his son-in-law Guillelmus de Orvalle and his wife Thomassia; Petrus Roulle, beadle; Conradus, illuminator; Robertus le Coustepointier and his wife Johanna; Richardus, beadle; Thomas Barsail; Guillelmus Calot Burgundus; Master Robertus Blondi; Radulphus Scriptor; frater Jacobus de Duaco, Mathurin; from 1300 to 1322 : Pierre Briffaut, beadle; Pierre Felisc.

The deeds give information on persons who received revenues on holdings in Clos-Bruneau between 1285 and 1299; Johannes de Volta; Canon Richardus Tesson; Philippus Carpentarius and his wife Alipdis; Master Arnandus Provincialis; Johannes de Campis, burgher; Arnulphus as Maillez; Guillelmus Bertrandi Canatarius; Guiardus de Latigniaco, burgher, and Johanna de Archiis, his wife; Master Arnaldus de Ambella and Nicolaa, his consort. Between 1300 and 1322 : Michael de Sancta-Susanna and his wife Johanna; Pelerin de Compigne; Baudet le Flament; around 1385 : Perrenelle la Riche, wife of Estienne le Riche.

The house bought by Emphastus (two buildings looking like one) was later called *domus Scarensis*, Hotel Suesse. After 1392 one part of Skara House was identified with the sign *Ymage de Nostre Dame*. The other part, which had no sign during the fifteenth century, was called *Maison du Cadran* towards the middle of the sixteenth. Skara House (Notre-Dame and *Maison du Cadran*) was adjacent to two other properties of the English-German Nation, *Petites Ecoles de Décret* and the house of Saint-Michel or *Double-Aigle*. The house Notre-Dame kept its name until the middle of the eighteenth century when we lose trace of it.

The approximate location of Skara House today would be between n°s 15 and 13 of Rue Jean-de-Beauvais, east of the square in front of the College of France.

The house of Emphastus, canon of Växjö, afterwards of Skara, later donated to the Chapter of Skara, survived four hundred years of adversities and remained a source of both worry and revenue for the English-German Nation. After the first quarter of the fifteenth century it lost its character as a hospice or college for Swedish students, but kept on its façade the image of the patron saint of the Cathedral Church of Skara, Our Lady, *Notre-Dame*.

PART III

CHARTULARY

The texts published in the Chartulary of this volume are preserved in a collection marked M 73 in the Archives Nationales, Paris. M 73 is a box, or *carton*, containing title deeds of the properties of the English-German Nation at the University of Paris. These deeds, mostly items of the sixteenth, seventeenth, and eighteenth centuries, are in bundles, or *liasses*.

Liasse A contains the deeds of the schools of the Nation : « Titres des Grandes et petites Ecolles de La Nation ou des Maisons de S. Charlemagne et du double Aigle, rue de Fouare. » In *Liasse B* are the eighteen documents edited here, the title deeds of the houses of Notre-Dame and Quadran, the Statutes of Skara House, and two receipts. (Cf. chapter I, note 1.) *Liasse C* has the title deeds of the houses of Saint-Michel and Petit Aigle, both located in rue « Saint »-Jean-de-Beauvais.

The eighteen deeds of *Liasse B* were numbered with Arabic numerals in the eighteenth century. But one document was not marked. A later hand renumbered the documents with Arabic numerals. Whenever the first number differs from the second one, I put the first number in brackets. The Roman numerals are mine, and are based upon the chronological order of the documents. Both enumerations, my Roman numerals and the Arabic numerals, are used in the footnotes in Parts I and II of the Book.

All the deeds in *Liasse B* are originals, written on parchment, except for n°s XVII and XVIII, which are on paper. Only n° XVI has been printed before.

The original spelling of the documents, including inconsistencies in the use of *t* and *c* and of *u* and *v* or *w*, has been preserved. Lest readers think errors in the text of the Chartulary are misprints, I have added [*sic*] even for obvious errors, and I have given, where necessary, the correct reading in notes. In capitalization and punctuation I have followed modern usage. Editorial additions are indicated by pointed brackets; illegible words reconstructed in the text are indicated by square brackets.

Explanatory notes concerning persons and places mentioned in the Chartulary can be found in parts I, *History*, and II, *Topography*, by means of the Index.

1284, January 13, Paris

Deed of the officialis of Guillelmus, archdeacon, and of the officialis of the Bishop of Paris, in which Johannes de Volta, son of Gillebertus, sells 6 sol. 9 den. annual rent to Richardus Tesson, clericus, for 7 libr. par., on a house [which later became the domus Scarensis, otherwise known as the house Ad Imaginem Nostre Domine] and grangia belonging to Guillelmus Biterne in Clos-Bruneau.

Vniuersis presentes litteras inspecturis, Parisiensis, et Guillelmi archdiaconi, Parisiensis ecclesie curiarum officiales, salutem in Domino. Noueritis quod in nostra presencia constitutus Johannes dictus de Volta clericus, filius quondam ut dicebat Gileberti de Volta, asseruit quod ipse super domo et grangia Guillelmi dicti 5 Biterne sibi ad inuicem contiguis et qualibet eorum insolidum sitis Parisius vltra Paruum Pontem in clauso Brunelli a parte superiori inter domum quondam Radolphi Scriptoris et domum Nicolai tallliatoris pannorum quarumdem dicta grangia est in censivis Sancti-Benedicti et domus in censivis Sancte-Genouefe, habebat et percipie- 10 bat jure hereditario sex solidos et nouem denarios paris. census incrementi annui redditus statim post fundus terre quatuor terminis Parisius consuetis annuatim.

Quos sex solidos et nouem denarios census et quicquid juris et actionis sibi in eis et in dictis domo et grangia eorum ratione com- 15 petebat, idem Johannes coram nobis recognouit se vendidisse et nomine venditionis ex nunc perpetuo quitauisse et concessisse magistro Richardo dicto Teisson clerico et eius heredibus siue ab ipso causam habituris pro precio sexaginta septem solidorum et sex denariorum paris. jam sibi soluto in pecunia numerata ut confessus 20 fuit coram nobis, renuncians per fidem exceptioni non numerati et non recepte pecunie predicte, ac promittens juramento prestito aduersus venditionem et quitationem huiusmodi non venire per se

uel alium jure aliquo in futurum et se dictos sex solidos et nouem
25 denarios census modo predicto annuatim imposterum libere capiendos super dictis domo et grangia quitos ab omni onere et obligatione
garantizaturum, liberaturum, et defensurum suis propriis sumptibus,
periculo et expensis in judicio et extra dicto emptori et eius heredibus siue ab eo causam habituris quandocumque opus fuerit contra
30 omnes et sibi pacifice solutorum tredecim solidos et sex denarios
paris. nomine pene seu interesse cum misiis et rectis costamentis si
dicta vendicio retracta fuerit in aliquo uel euicta et quantum ad hec
et pro recta garandia ferenda.

Idem venditor se et heredes suos et omnia bona sua et heredum
35 suorum mobilia et immobilia presentia et futura tituloque speciali
ypotheca dimidium arpentum vinee quod dicebat se habere apud
Arcolium in censivis Sancti-Dionisii et Sancti-Eligii dicto emptori
et ab eo causam habituris obligauit et se quantum ad hec jurisdictioni supradictarum curiarum nostrarum supposuit. In cuius rei
40 testimonium sigilla dictarum curiarum duximus hiis litteris apponendum.

Datum anno Domini M⁰ CC⁰ LXXX⁰ tertio, die Jouis post Epi-
phaniam Domini.

Durandus

Parchment : 177 × 166 mm.
Two seals on tags.
*Endorsements : 1) « Carta Johannis de Volta, clerici, pro sex
solidis et novem denariis paris. » (Late thirteenth-century hand);
2) « Inventorié XIX » (Eighteenth-century hand).*

1285, February 6, Paris

Paris, Arch. Nat.,
M 73, n° 2

Deed of the officialis of Guillelmus, archdeacon, and of the offi-
cialis of the Bishop of Paris, containing the sale of 14 sol. par. rent
on a house of Guillelmus Biterne and his wife Johanna, located
in Clos-Bruneau [domus Scarensis], by Philippus Carpentarius
and Alipdis, his wife, to Richardus Tesson, canon of Paris, for
7 libr. par.

Vniuersis presentes litteras inspecturis Parisiensis, et Guillermi
archidiaconi, in ecclesia Parisiensi curiarum officiales, salutem in
Domino. Noueritis quod coram nobis personaliter constituti Philippus Carpentarius et Alipdis eius vxor asseruerunt coram nobis quod
ipsi coniuges habebant, capiebant et leuabant annis singulis quatuor 5
terminis Parisius consuetis quatuordecim solidos paris. augmentati
census seu redditus annui super quandam domum Guillermi dicti
Biterne clerici et Johanne eius vxoris sitam Parisius ultra Paruum
Pontem in clauso Bunelli [1]) [*sic*], contiguam ex vna parte domui
Nicholai cisoris pannorum, et ex altera cuidam alteri domui ipsorum 10
Guillermi et eius vxoris; quos siquidem quatuordecim solidos paris.
annui census seu redditus prefati Philippus et eius vxor recognouerunt et confessi fuerunt coram nobis se vendidisse et nomine pure
venditionis et simplicis concessisse et in perpetuum quittauisse vene-
rabili viro et discreto magistro Richardo dicto Tesson Parisiensi 15
canonico et eius heredibus et causam habituris ab eodem pro precio
septem librarum paris. sibi solutarum et traditarum pre manibus a
predicto canonico in pecunia numerata, exceptioni dicte summe pecunie non solute, non numerate et non tradite renunciantes penitus
et expresse.   20
   Promiseruntque dicti venditores fide et juramento prestitis corpo-
ralibus ab eisdem quod contra huiusmodi venditionem, concessionem

---

1) Brunelli.

et quitationem per se uel per alium non venient in futurum nec venire procurabunt et quod ipsi venditores predictos quatuordecim
25 solidos paris. annui census seu redditus predicto canonico et causam habituris ab eodem garantizabunt, liberabunt et defendent in judicio et extra ad usus et consuetudines Francie suis propriis sumptibus et expensis contra omnes quocienscumque opus fuerit et super hoc fuerint requisiti.
30 Obligauerunt etiam dicti venditores dicto emptori et causam habituris ab eodem quantum ad hec se heredesque suos bona sua heredumque suorum mobilia et immobilia presentia et futura in quibuscumque locis et rebus existant et poterint inueniri.
Necnon voluerunt et expresse concesserunt predicti venditores
35 coram nobis quod si contingerit predictos quatuordecim solidos paris. annui census seu redditus vt premissum est dicto canonico venditos retrahi vel euici in aliquo quod ipsi venditores uel eorum heredes quintum denarios nomine pene dicto emptori aut causam habituris ab eodem cum expensis et interesse quas et quod propter
40 hoc incurrerint aut sustinuerint soluere teneantur, renunciantes in hoc facto exceptioni doli mali, actioni in factum priuilegio crucis sumpte et assumende, petitioni libelli et copie presentis instrumenti et ne possint dicere in premissis se fuisse deceptos seu etiam circonuentos necnon et dicta Aalipdis per prestitum juramentum excep-
45 tioni a uelleyani et omnibus aliis exceptionibus juris et facti que contra presens instrumentum possent obici seu dici et que dicto emptori et causam habituris ab eodem possent abesse in premissis uel aliquo premissorum et dictis venditoribus seu eorum heredibus prodesse necnon et juris dicenti generalem renunciationem non
50 valere, jurisdictionibus curiarum nostrarum quantum ad hec se supponentes vbicumque se duxerint transferendos se nichilominus de predictis quatuordecim solidis paris. annui census seu redditus penitus deuestientes et desaisientes et predictum canonicum per traditionem presentis instrumenti saisientes et in possessionem po-
55 nentes.
In cuius rei testimonium sigillum curiarum nostrarum presentibus litteris duximus apponendum. Datum anno Domini M° CC° octogesimo quarto, die Martis post festum Purificationis beate Marie Virginis.

Parchment : 264 × 258 mm.
Tags for two seals. [One seal is missing].

Endorsements : 1) « Quitacio .xiiij. sol. paris. pro domo Sca-rensi, Rihardi [?] Tesson » (Late thirteenth-century hand);
2) « Vieulx lettres faisant mention des maisons en la rue de St. Jean de Beauvais appartenantes à la nation d'Allemagne » (Eighteenth-century hand n° I);
3) « Ces maisons sont celle du Quadran et de St. Michel * contigues et qui se doivent aboutir par derrier à la ruelle sans teste ou bien à la rue Josselin en la censive ou seigneurie de Ste Genevieve » (Eight-eenth-century hand n° II); marginal note in a third hand (n° III) : * « Ce titre est mal mis », apparently referring to the words « St. Michel », marked with an asterisk. The same hand (n° III) conti-nues : « Ce n'est point icy les titres d'amortissement de ces maisons, mais la vente d'une rente. L'une d'icelle qui fut rachetée ensuitte. Voyez num. 5 ». In the same hand under a cross : « ces maisons sont celles du Quadran et de Notre-Dame, anciennement appelée Domus Scarensis ou Hostel de Swecie. La maison de St. Michel ne fut acquise qu'en l'an 1415 » (Eighteenth-century hand n° III);
4) « Inventorié XII » (Eighteenth-century hand n° IV).

III

1288, December 20, Paris   Paris, Arch. Nat.,
                                                    M 73, nº 3

Deed of the officialis of Guillelmus, archdeacon of Paris, in which Thomas Tyha, clericus, and Isabellis, his wife, daughter of the late Guillelmus Biterne, renounce their properties, inherited from her parents, in favor of Guillelmus de Orvalle and Thomassia, his wife, daughter of Guillelmus Biterne.

Vniuersis presentes litteras inspecturis officialis curie Guillelmi ecclesie Parisiensis archidiaconi salutem in Domino. Notum facimus quod coram nobis constituti Thomas de Tyha clericus et Ysabellis eius vxor, filia defuncti Guillelmi dicti Biterne, voluntate
5 spontanea non coacta sed ex certa scientia quitauerunt, cesserunt et remiserunt penitus perpetuo et omnino specialiter et expresse ac per fidem Guillelmo de Orualle clerico et Thomassie eius vxori ac eorum heredibus omnia et singula bona hereditaria et immobilia existencia tam in terris, vineis, pratis, domibus et ortis quam in
10 aliis possessionibus quibuscumque quecumque et vbicumque sint et fuerint et quocumque nomine censeantur que ipse Guillelmus Biterne et Johanna quondam eius vxor habebant, tenebant et possidebant tempore quo viuebant tam jure hereditario quam ratione conquestus seu alio quoque jure tam quicquid juris et actionis, dominii, pro-
15 prietatis et possessionis ipsi Thomas et Ysabellis habebant et habere poterant ac debebant ratione seu causa quacumque in eisdem et quolibet eorundem nichil juris vel actionis in eis sibi vel suis heredibus retinentes et fide dicta promittentes quod contra hec jure aliquo per se aut per alium non venient in futurum et quod in eis
20 bonis nichil juris vel actionis decetero reclamabunt nisi eis obuenerit ex successione dicte Ysabellis.
Dum tamen ipsi Guillelmus et Thomassia teneantur aquitare erga omnes dictos Thomam et Ysabellam ac heredes eorum super omnibus bonis, rebus et debitis ac creditis in quibus tenebantur dicti
25 Guillelmus Biterne et eius <vxor> tempore quo viuebant credi-

130

toribus quibuscumque et ea soluere ac indempnes obseruare erga omnes.

Preterea dicti Guillelmus de Orualle et Thomassia coram nobis constituti premissa voluerunt, laudauerunt et acceptauerunt ac complere promiserunt fide data et de non veniendo contra fidem de- 30 derunt.

Datum anno Domini M° CC° octuagesimo octauo die Lune ante Nativitatem Domini.

Parchment : 206 × 142 mm.
Fragments of seal on tag.
Endorsement : « Jacobus Hure, Johanna uxor, filia Biterne »
(Late thirteenth-century hand).

IV

1292, January 8, Paris

Paris, Arch. Nat.,
M 73, nᵒ 4

*Deed of the officialis of the Bishop of Paris, in which Jacobus
Hure and his wife Johanna, daughter of the late Guillelmus Biterne,
renounce all the properties which they inherited from Guillelmus
Biterne and his wife, in favor of Guillelmus de Orvalle and his
wife Thomassia.*

Vniuersis presentes litteras inspecturis officialis curie Parisiensis salutem in Domino. Notum facimus quod coram nobis in jure
constituti Jacobus dictus Hure et Johanna eius vxor, filia defuncti
Guillelmi Biterne, voluntate spontanea non coacta sed ex certa
5 scientia quitauerunt, cesserunt et remiserunt penitus et perpetuo,
expresse et per fidem Guillelmo de Orualle clerico et Thomassie
eius vxori ac eorum heredibus omnia et singula bona hereditaria et
immobilia existencia tam in terris, vineis, pratis, domibus et ortis
quam in aliis possessionibus quibuscumque quecumque et vbicum-
10 que sint et fuerint et quocumque nomine censeantur que ipse Guillelmus Biterne et Johanna quondam eius vxor habebant, tenebant et
possidebant tempore quo viuebant tam jure hereditario quam ratione
conquestus seu alio quoque jure et quicquid juris et actionis, dominii, proprietatis, possessionis ipsi Jacobus et Johanna habebant
15 et habere poterant ac debebant ratione seu causa quacumque in
eisdem et in quolibet eorumdem, nichil juris vel actionis sibi et suis
heredibus in eis retinentes et fide data promittentes quod contra
hec, jure aliquo per se aut per alium non venient in futurum, et
quod in eisdem bonis nichil juris vel actionis decetero reclamabunt
20 nisi eis obuenerit ex successione dicte Johanne ita tamen quod dicti
Guillelmus et Thomassia teneantur aquitare erga omnes dictos
Jacobum et Johannam ac heredes eorum super omnibus bonis rebus
et debitis ac creditis in quibus tenebantur dicti Guillelmus Biterne
et eius vxor tempore quo viuebant personis et creditoribus quibus-
25 cumque et ea soluere ac eos indempnes penitus super hiis obser-

uare erga omnes suis propriis sumptibus erga omnes eciam personas.

Preterea dicti Guillelmus de Orualle et Thomassia coram nobis constituti premissa voluerunt, laudauerunt et acceptauerunt ac complere promiserunt fide data et eos Jacobum et Johannam liberare et 30 idempnes obseruare super omnibus antedictis erga omnes obligare eis quantum ad hec se et heredes suos et omnia sua bona et quilibet eorum insolidum et per fidem.

Datum anno Domini M° CC° nonagesimo primo die Martis post festum Epiphanie Domini.   35

Parchment : 256 × 172 mm.
Tag for seal. [Seal missing.]
Endorsement : « Inventorié XVII » (Eighteenth-century hand).

V

1292, September 10, Paris

Paris, Arch. Nat.,
M 73, n° 5

*Deed of the officialis of the Bishop of Paris, in which Guillelmus
de Orvalle and his wife Thomassia sell two contiguous houses with
a court and garden [domus Scarensis] to Emphastus, canon of the
diocese of Wexio [Växjö] in Sweden, for 60 libr. par. The houses
were situated in Clos-Bruneau in the censives of Sainte-Geneviève,
Saint-Benoît, and Saint-Marcel. The houses were charged with a
yearly cens of 105 sol. 1 den. paris. : that is, 26 sol. due to Saint-
Benoît; 32 sol. to master Arnandus; 11 sol. 8 den. to Johannes de
Campis, burgher of Paris; 5 sol. 10 den. to Arnulphus as Maillez;
8 sol. 9 den. to Guillelmus [Bertrandi] Canatarius; and 20 sol.
10 den. to master Richardus Tesson.*

Vniuersis presentes litteras inspecturis officialis curie Parisiensis
salutem in Domino. Notum facimus quod in presentia nostra constituti Guillelmus dictus de Orualle et Thomasia eius vxor, filia
quondam Guillelmi dicti Biterne bedelli defuncti, asserentes se ex
5 propria hereditate dicte Thomassie habere, tenere et possidere duas
domos sibi ad inuicem attinentes sitas Parisius vltra Paruum Pontem
in clauso Burnelli, contiguas ex vno latere domui Guillelmi dicti
Calot et cuidam domui quae quondam fuit defuncti magistri Roberti
Blondi et ex alio latere cuidam alii domui ipsorum coniugum cum
10 quadam curte seu jardineto retro dictam domum ipsorum coniugum separato et diuiso a dicta eorum domo et aliam domum eidem
contiguam ut predicitur pertinente, contiguas insuper a parte
posteriori et attinentes cuidam domui quae quondam fuit Mathei
de Orto Lombardi ex parte vna, et domui magistri Petri de Villa
15 Blouana clerici, seque protendunt dicte domus vt dicebant a dicta
parte posteriori vsque ad quemdam vicum seu ruellam sine capite
appellatum vicus [*sic*] Jocelini in dominiis seu censiuis sanctorum
Genouefe, Benedicti Parisius et Marcelli, oneratas in vniuerso in

134

centum et quinque solidis et vno denario paris. vt dicebant tantum-
modo annui census seu perpetui redditus debitis annuatim personis 20
infrascriptis : videlicet ecclesie Sancti Benedicti predicti viginti
sex solidos; magistro Arnando provinciali triginta duos solidos;
Johanni de Campis ciui Parisiensi vndecim solidos et octo denarios; Arnulpho dicto as Maillez sex solidos duobus denariis minus;
item Guillelmo Canaterio octo solidos et nouem denarios; item 25
magistro Richardo dicto Tesson viginti vno solidos duobus denariis
minus.

Ipsas duas domos cum curte seu jardineto predicto cum omnibus
aliis suis appendiciis et pertinentiis prout se comportant ante et
retro, in longo et lato, inferius et superius, cum omni jure, dominio 30
et proprietate dictis coniugibus in eisdem domibus competentibus,
recognouerunt in jure coram nobis dicti coniuges se pro se [suisque
heredibus] vendidisse et nomine pure ac simplicis venditionis ex
nunc imperpetuum cessisse, quitauisse et concessisse discreto viro
domino Emphasto canonico Wexyonensi de regno Swecie eiusque 35
heredibus seu causam ab ipso habituris pro sexaginta libris paris.
eisdem coniugibus a predicto emptore jam traditis et solutis in pecunia numerata, vt dicti coniuges in jure coram nobis sunt confessi,
et de quibus se tenuerunt coram nobis pro bene pagatis et contentis.

Cedentes jam dicti coniuges predicto Emphasto eiusque heredibus 40
et causam ab ipso habituris ac in eosdem omnino ex nunc imperpetuum transferentes et a se totaliter abdicantes omne jus, dominium
omnemque proprietatem, causam et actionem realem et personalem,
vtilem, directam, tacitam et expressam atque mixtam necnon et
possessionem que eisdem venditoribus in predictis duabus domibus, 45
curte et earum pertinentibus competebant et competere poterant et
debebant quoquo modo nichil juris, dominii, proprietatis, cause,
actionis seu possessionis ipsis coniugibus vel eorum heredibus in
dictis domibus et earum pertinentibus decetero retinendo.

Et promiserunt jamdicti venditores fide ab ipsis in manu nostra 50
prestita corporali quod contra venditionem, concessionem, quitationem, cessionem et translationem predictas jure hereditario, ratione
conquestus, dotis, doarii, dotalicii seu donationis, propter nuptias
aut alio quouis jure communi uel speciali per se uel per alium seu
alios non venient aut venire facient uel procurabunt alioquatenus 55
in futurum; et quod ipsi venditores suprascripti duas domos cum
curte et omnibus aliis earum pertinentibus prout se comportant et
protendunt, vt superius est expressum, eidem emptori, eiusque heredibus et causam ab ipso habituris, ipsorum coniugum propriis sump-

60 tibus, periculo et expensis garantizabunt, liberabunt et defendent in judicio et extra quociens opus fuerit ad vsus et consuetudines parisienses contra omnes; necnon quod reddent et soluent eidem emptori duodecim libras paris. nomine pene si dicta venditio in toto vel in parte a quoquam retracta fuerit seu etiam euicta, cum restauratione 65 plenaria omnium aliorum dampnorum, interesse et expensarum si quae uel quas dictus emptor ob defectum garantizationis predicte seu eius occasione faceret, incureret uel haberet, credendo super hiis simplici juramento emptoris eiusdem.

Obligantes quantum ad hec dicti venditores eidem emptori et 70 causam ab ipso habituris se heredesque suos et specialiter in contraplegium quasdam scolas quas se habere dicebant et tenere sitas in clauso Brunelli predicto, contiguas ex parte vna domui Petri Roulle bedelli, et ex parte alia scolis Conradi illuminatoris, ac censum et redditum scolarum earumdem, omniaque alia sua, et 75 heredum suorum bona mobilia et inmobilia presentia et futura vbicumque et in quibuscumque rebus et locis existentia seque jurisdictioni Parisiensi curie supponentes.

Et in hoc facto sub virtute jam prestite fidei renunciantes exceptioni pecunie predicte non numerate et non recepte pecunie speique 80 future numerationis ac rei non sit geste fori et crucis assumpte et assumende, priuilegio omnique lesioni, deceptioni et circumuentioni.

Et ne possint dicere uel opponere in futurum se in contractu huiusmodi ultra medietatem justi precii lesos esse uel fuisse seu deceptos aut in aliquo circumuentos omnique alii juri et facti 85 auxilio canonici et ciuilis, juri etiam dicent generalem renunciationem non valere.

In cuius rei testimonium ad petitionem suprascriptorum coniugum sigillum curie Parisiensis litteris presentibus duximus apponendum. Datum anno Domini millesimo ducentesimo nonagesimo secundo, 90 die Mercurii post festum Nativitatis beate Marie virginis.

Benedictus de Londoniis.

Parchment : 260 × 301 mm.
Tag for seal.
Endorsements : 1) « Thomasine littera venditionis domus [....] domino Hemfasto » (Late thirteenth-century hand);
2) « Litere domus Almanorum ad Insigne Quadrantis » (Late sixteenth-century hand);

136

3) « Titre principal de l'acquisition de deux maisons au Clos Brunel Rue Saint Jean de Beauvais à la Nation d'Alemagne par M. Emphaste, chanoine Suédois au mois de Septembre 1292.

« Les autres titres cy attachées sont des rachats de rentes sus lesdittes maisons fait par ledict Emphaste.

« Ces maisons sont celles du Quadran et de Notre Dame car la 3ᵉ maison de St. Michel ou de l'Aigle ne fut acquis qu'en l'an 1415 comme il parait par le contract d'achat parmi les titres de la Nation.

« Il y avoit autrefois en ces maisons appellées Domus Scaren. une communauté d'Allemans ou Suédois dont il y les statuts parmi les titres. » (Eighteenth-century hand nᵒ I);
4) « Inventorié XV » (Eighteenth-century hand nᵒ II).

1292, December 9, Paris

*Deed of the officialis of the Bishop of Paris, in which Robertus
Coustepointier and his wife Johanna sell 26 sol. annual cens on a
house located in Clos-Bruneau between the schools of Richardus the
beadle and those of Guillelmus de Orvalle in the censive of the
Bishop of Paris, to Emphastus, canon of the diocese of Wexio
[Växjö] in Sweden, for 9 libr. par.*

    Vniuersis presentes litteras inspecturis officialis curie Parisien-
sis salutem in Domino. Notum facimus quod in presentia nostra
personaliter propter hoc constituti Robertus dictus le Coustepointier
et Johanna eius vxor asserentes se ex eorum proprio conquestu
5 habere, percipere, leuare et recipere singulis annis super quadam
domo sita Parisius vltra Paruum Pontem in vico Clausi Brunelli in
censiua domini Parisiensis episcopi, contigua ex vna parte domui
et scolis Richardi bedelli, et ex alia parte scolis Guillelmi de Orualle
clerici generalis olim Guillelmi Biterne, et a parte posteriori domui
10 Thome Bursail, que quidem domus quondam fuit Guiardi de Latigniaco ciuis et Johanne de Archiis quondam eius eius [*sic*] vxoris,
viginti et sex solidos paris. annui augmentati census seu perpetui
redditus quatuor terminis Parisius generaliter consuetis inmediate
post quatuor libras et quatuordecim solidos paris. in quibus dicta
15 domus erat primitus onerata tam ratione capitalis census debiti
domino Parisiensi episcopo quam etiam augmentatis aliis censua-
rie debitis, recognouerunt et confessi sunt coram nobis sua spontanea voluntate et ex certa sciencia se pro se suisque heredibus
predictos viginti et sex solidos paris. annui augmentati census
20 et quicquid juris et actionis eisdem coniugibus in dicto censu et
domo predicta ratione census eiusdem competebat et competere
poterat et debebat, vendidisse et nomine pure ac simplicis venditionis ex nunc imperpetuum cessisse, quitavisse et concessisse

discreto viro domino Emphasto canonico Wexyonensi et eius
heredibus seu causam ab ipso habituris pro nouem libris paris., 25
eisdem coniugibus a jam dicto canonico traditis et solutis in pecunia numerata.

Et de quibus se tenuerunt coram nobis in solidum pro bene pagatis et contentis, exceptioni non numerate, non habite, nec recepte
pecunie penitus et per fidem renunciando. 30

Promittentes dicti venditores fide ab ipsis in manu nostra prestita
corporali quod contra venditionem, cessionem, quitationem et concessionem predictas jure hereditario, ratione conquestus, dotis, doarii, dotalicii, donationis, propter nuptias aut alio quouis jure communi uel speciali per se uel per alium non venient aut venire facient 35
uel procurabunt aliquatenus in futurum immo quod ipsi venditores
predictos viginti sex solidos paris. annui augmentati census habendos, tenendos, leuandos et percipiendos a predicto emptore eiusque
heredibus seu causam ab ipso habituris super totali domo predicta
et eius pertinentibus, prout se comportat inmediate post quatuor 40
libras et quatuordecim solidos paris. ut predicitur, in quibus dicta
domus primitus est et erat onerata quatuor terminis Parisius ut superius est expressum consuetis ex nunc imperpetuum dicto canonico
eiusque heredibus et causam ab ipso habituris ipsorum venditorum
propriis sumptibus, periculo et expensis absque omni onere, impe- 45
dimento et obligatione quibuscumque garantizabunt, liberabunt et
defendent in judicio et extra quociens opus fuerit ad vsus et consuetudines Parisienses contra omnes. Necnon quod reddent et soluent
dicto emptori seu causam ab ipso habituris triginta et sex solidos
paris. nomine pene si dicta venditio a quoquam retracta fuerit seu 50
etiam euicta cum omnibus aliis rectis, misiis, costamentis, interesse
et expensis que et quas dictus emptor seu eius mandatum per suum
simplex juramentum absque alio probationis onere se ob defectum
garantizationis predicte ferende modo quo supra fecisse, habuisse
diceret aut modo quolibet incurrisse. 55

Obligantes quantum ad hoc prenominati coniuges eidem domino
Emphasto eiusque heredibus et causam ab ipso habituris se et
heredes suos omnia sua et heredum suorum bona mobilia et immobilia presentia et futura vbicumque et in quibuscumque rebus
et locis existentia, et ex nunc in contraplegium pro permissis obli- 60
gatis eisdem reliquerunt et se jurisdictioni Parisiensis curie supposuerunt.

In cuius rei testimonium ad petitionem dictorum coniugum sigillum curie Parisiensis litteris presentibus duximus apponendum.

65 Datum anno Domini millesimo ducentesimo nonagesimo secundo, die Martis post hyemale festum beati Nicolai.

Benedictus de Londoniis.

Parchment : 230 × 295 mm.
Fragments of seal on tag.
Endorsements : 1) « Littera census redemptionis . . . xxvj . sol. Robertus [Coustepointier] » (Late thirteenth-century hand);
2) « Inventorié XIX » (Eighteenth-century hand).

VII

1293, February 4, Paris

Paris, Arch. Nat.,
M 73, n° 7

Deed of the officialis of the Bishop of Paris, in which Richardus Tesson, canon of Paris, sells 20 sol. and 10 den. annual cens on two contiguous houses [domus Scarensis] in Clos-Bruneau in the censives of Sainte-Geneviève, Saint-Benoît, and Saint-Marcel, to Emphastus, canon of the diocese of Wexio [Växjö] in Sweden, for 20 libr. tur.

Vniuersis presentes litteras inspecturis officialis curie Parisiensis salutem in Domino. Notum facimus quod in presencia nostra constitutus venerabilis vir magister Richardus dictus Tesson canonicus Parisiensis asseruit coram nobis quod ipse ex suo proprio conquestu habebat, tenebat et possidebat ac leuebat et percipiebat 5 singulis annis quatuor terminis Parisius generaliter consuetis viginti solidos et decem denarios paris. annui census seu perpetui redditus super duabus domibus sibi ad inuicem attinentibus sitis Parisius ultra Paruum Pontem in Clauso Burnelli contiguis ex vno latere domui Guillelmi dicti Calot et cuidam domui que quondam fuit 10 defuncti magistri Roberti Blondi, et ex alio latere domui Guillelmi dicti de Orualle et Thomasie eius vxoris filie quondam Guillelmi dicti Biterne bedelli defuncti, prout se comportant, in dominiis seu censiuis sanctorum Genouefe et Benedicti Parisius ac Sancti Marcelli juxta Parisios. 15

Quos siquidem viginti solidos cum decem denariis paris. annui census seu redditus idem magister Richardus recognouit et confessus est in jure se pro se suisque heredibus vendidisse et nomine pure ac simplicis venditionis ex nunc imperpetuum cessisse, quitauisse et concessisse cum omni jure, dominio, proprietate, causa, actione et posses- 20 sione que eidem magistro in ipso censu seu reddito competebant et competere poterant et debebant necnon et in dictis domibus ratione census eiusdem discreto viro domino Emphasto canonico Wexyonensi de regno Swecie eiusque heredibus seu causam ab ipso habituris

141

25 pro viginti libris turon. dicto magistro Richardo ab ipso domino
Emphasto solutis et deliberatis in pecunia numerata, vt idem venditor in jure coram nobis est confessus, et de quibus se tenuit coram
nobis pro bene pagato, exceptioni non numerate et non recepte
pecunie ac rei non sit geste penitus et expresse renunciando.

30   Promittens bona fide quod contra venditionem, quitationem,
cessionem et concessionem predictas quoquo jure communi uel
speciali aut ingenio seu cautela quacumque per se uel per alium
seu alios non veniet aut venire faciet uel procurabit aliquotenus in
futurum. Et quod ipse dictos viginti solidos cum decem denariis
35 paris. annui census seu perpetui redditus habendos, tenendos et
possidendos ex nunc imperpetuum super domibus predictis ab ipso
emptore et eius heredibus quatuor terminis Parisius ut premittitur
consuetis dicto emptori et eius heredibus seu causam ab ipso habituris garantizabit, liberabit et defendet ipsius venditoris propriis
40 sumptibus et expensis in judicio et extra quociens opus fuerit et
super hoc extiterit requisitus ad vsus et consuetudines Parisienses
contra omnes; se quantum ad hec heredesque suos omnia sua et
heredum suorum bona mobilia et immobilia, presentia et futura,
vbicumque existentia seque jurisdictioni Parisiensis curie suppo-
45 nendo et specialiter et expresse emptori predicto et eius heredibus
obligando. In cuius rei testimonium ad peticionem dicti magistri
Richardi sigillum curie Parisiensis litteris presentibus duximus
apponendum.
   Datum anno Domini millesimo ducentesimo nonagesimo secundo,
50 die Mercurii post festum Purificationis beate Marie Virginis.

Benedictus de Londoniis.

Parchment : 210 × 240 mm.
Tag for seal. [Seal missing.]
*Endorsements : 1) « Littera venditionis census super . xx . sol.
cum . x . den. de magistro Richardo dicto Tesson » (Late thirteenth-century hand) ;*
2) « Inventorié XVIII » (Eighteenth-century hand).

142

VIII

1298, July 19, Paris   Paris, Arch. Nat.,
                                        M 73, n° 8

*Deed of the officialis of the Bishop of Paris, in which master
Arnaldus de Ambella and his wife Nicolaa sell 40 sol. tur. annual
cens on two contiguous houses [domus Scarensis] in Clos-Bruneau,
to Emphastus, rector of the church of Falköping, for 24 libr. par.*

Vniuersis presentes litteras inspecturis officialis curie Parisiensis salutem in Domino. Notum facimus quod in nostra presentia
magister Arnaldus de Ambella et coram Benedicto dicto de Londoniis et Johanne dicto ad Dentem clerico curie nostre, notariis
juratis ad hec a nobis specialiter destinatis et deputatis quibus in 5
hiis et in maioribus fidem plenariam adhibemus, Nicolaa predicti
magistri Arnaldi vxor constituti asserentes se ex dicti magistri
proprio conquestu percipere, tenere, habere et possidere super duas
domos que pro una reputantur et habentur que quondam fuerunt
Guillelmi dicti Bisterne et Gileberti dicti de Vouta, sitas ultra 10
Paruum Pontem sibi ad inuicem attinentes contiguas ex vno latere
domui Guillelmi dicti Calot et cuidam domui que quondam fuit
defuncti magistri Roberti Blondi, et ex alio latere cuidam domui
Guillelmi dicti de Orualle et Thomasie eius vxoris prout undique
se comportant quadraginta solidos turon. annui census seu perpetui 15
redditus quatuor terminis Parisius generaliter consuetis : dictos quadraginta solidos turon. annui census seu perpetui redditus cum omne
jure, dominio, et proprietate dictis coniugibus in eisdem ac etiam
in prescriptis domibus ratione dicti census seu redditus competentibus recognouerunt, et in ueritate confessi fuerunt se pro se suisque 20
heredibus vendidisse et nomine pure ac simplicis venditionis ex
nunc imperpetuum cessisse, quitauisse et concessisse domino Hemphasto rectori ecclesie Phalocopensis de regno Swecie eiusque heredibus seu causam ab eo habituris pro viginti quatuor libris paris.
ipsis coniugibus a dicto rectore jam traditis et solutis in pecunia 25
numerata vt idem magister coram nobis et eius vxor coram predictis

143

juratis nostris recognouerunt et sunt confessi, et de quibus se tenuerunt pro bene pagatis et contentis, cedentes jam dicti coniuges pre-
nominato Hemphasto eiusque heredibus et ab eo causam habituris,
30 ac in eosdem ex nunc imperpetuum transferentes quicquid juris, dominii, proprietatis, cause, possessionis et actionis realis et personalis,
utilis, directe, tacite et expresse atque mixte ipsis coniugibus in
predictis quadraginta solidos turon. annui census seu perpetui
redditus necnon in domo seu domibus predictis et earum pertinen-
35 tiis, situatis ultra Paruum Pontem ut pretactum est videlicet in
Clauso Burnelli et que domus ad dictum emptorem jure dominii
dicuntur spectare et pertinere, competebat et competere poterat et
debebat ratione dicti census quoque modo nichil juris, dominii,
proprietatis, cause, actionis uel possessionis ipsis venditoribus uel
40 eorum heredibus in predicto censu seu redditu aut in domo seu
domibus predictis causa et occasione dicti census seu redditus decetero retinendo.

Et promiserunt dicti coniuges scilicet prefatus magister Arnaldus
in manu nostra et prenominata Nicolaa eius vxor in manibus
45 prescriptorum juratorum nostrorum fide prestita corporali quod
contra venditionem, cessionem, quitationem et translationem predictas jure hereditario, ratione conquestus, dotis, doarii, dotalicii,
donationis, propter nuptias aut alio quouis jure communi uel speciali
per se uel per alium seu alios non venient nec venire facient uel
50 procurabunt aliquatenus in futurum; et quod ipsi venditores predicti suprascriptum annuum censum seu perpetuum redditum quadraginta solidorum turon. modo et forma prenotatis venditorum
predicto emptori absque omni impedimento et obligatione quibuscumque garantizabunt, liberabunt et defendent in judicio et extra
55 quociens opus fuerit et super hoc extiterint requisiti ad vsus et
consuetudines Parisienses contra omnes.

Obligantes quantum ad hec dicti venditores prefato emptori se
et heredes suos omnia sua et heredum suorum bona, mobilia et immobilia, presentia et futura, vbicumque et in quibuscumque rebus
60 et locis existentia, jurisdictionique Parisiensis curie specialiter et
expresse supponentes, et in hoc facto sub uirtute jam prestite fidei
renunciantes omnem exceptionem doli, lesionis, deceptionis, et
circumuentionis cuiuslibet, reique sic non geste fori et crucis
priuilegio, appellationis remedio et omni alii juri et facti auxilio,
65 canonico et civili juri etiam dicenti generalem renunciationem non
ualere; necnon et mulier predicta omni juri ob fauorem mulierem
introducto.

In quorum omnium testimonium sigillum curie Parisiensis ad petitionem sepedicti magistri Arnaldi et ad relationem juratorum nostrorum predictorum litteris presentibus duximus apponendum. 70

Datum anno Domini millesimo ducentesimo nonagesimo octauo, die Sabbati ante festum beate Marie Magdalene.

Per Benedictum de Londoniis.

Parchment : 242 × 290 mm.
Seal on tag.
Endorsements : 1) « Quitacio . xl . sol. Turon. a magistro Arnalto » (Late thirteenth-century hand);
2) « Titre d'une maison » (Late sixteenth-century hand);
3) « Inventorié XVIII » (Eighteenth-century hand).

IX

1299, September 10, Paris   Paris, Arch. Nat.,
M 73, n° 9

Statement made before the officialis of the Bishop of Paris by Guillelmus Calot, acknowledging that the fact that Emphastus, rector of the church of Falköping in Sweden, had voluntarily repaired the wall between his house and that of Guillelmus did not establish a precedent and that Guillelmus and his heirs would still be obligated to repair their half of the wall whenever it became necessary.

Vniuersis presentes litteras inspecturis officialis curie Parisiensis salutem in Domino. Notum facimus quod in nostra propter hoc presentia personaliter constitutus Guillelmus dictus Calot Burgundus asserens se habere et possidere quamdam domum sitam Pari-
5 sius ultra Paruum Pontem in Clauso Burnelli in censiua Sancti Benedicti Parisiensis, contiguam ex parte una domui fratris Jacobi de Duaco ordinis Sancti Maturini et ex parte alia contiguam et attinentem cuidam domui discreti viri domini Hemphasti rectoris ecclesie Phalocopensis de regno Swetie scolaris Parisiensis.
10 Asserens etiam murum medium inter dictas duas domos esse medietarium et communem inter dictum rectorem ex parte una et dictum Guillelmum ex alia, dictumque murum euidenti et necessaria reparatione indigere, et se paupertate oppressum non posse partem ipsum contingentem in reparatione huiusmodi apponere.
15 Recognouit et confessus est coram nobis quod prefatus dominus Hemphastus ex sua mera liberalitate et gratia speciali et in remunerationem quorundam seruiciorum dicto H<emphasto> ab ipso ut asserebat impensorum, dictum murum suis propriis sumptibus et expensis construi et reparari facit et proponit. Nolens dictus Guil-
20 lelmus nec intendens quod per constructionem seu reparationem huiusmodi aliquod imposterum dicto domino Hemphasto, eius successoribus aut ab eo causam habit<ur>is quoad dictum murum construendum et reparandum processu temporis cum necesse fuerit

preiudicium generetur quin dictus Guillelmus, eius heredes et
successores in ipso domo dictum murum construere pro media parte 25
et reparare de cetero teneantur, et quod per constructionem seu
reparationem huiusmodi quam idem dominus H<emphastus> ad
presens ex sua gratia speciali ut pretactum est et de pecunia sua
propria facit, dicto Guillelmo, eius heredibus seu successoribus aliquid juris nullatenus acquiratur uel accrescat. Inmo dictus murus 30
prout hactenus extitit communis inter ipsos et medietarius imposterum remaneat et existat. In cuius rei testimonium sigillum curie
Parisiensis litteris presentibus duximus apponendum.

Datum anno Domini millesimo ducentesimo nonagesimo nono,
die Jouis post festum Nativitatis beate Marie Virginis. 35

Benedictus de Londoniis.

Parchment : 230 × 175 mm.
Seal on tag.
Endorsements : 1) « De muro intermedio » (Early fourteenth-
century hand);
2) « D'une maison au Clos-Bruneau » (Late sixteenth-century
hand);
3) « Inventorié XIX » (Eighteenth-century hand).
4) « Inventorié XXV » (Eighteenth-century hand n° II).

X

1300, August 7, Paris   Paris, Arch. Nat.,
                                                   M 73, n° 11

The dean and the Chapter of Saint-Marcel transfer to Emphastus,
rector of the church of Falköping in Sweden, a small house next to
the house of Emphastus in Clos-Bruneau, for a yearly cens of
5 sol. par., payable twice a year, i.e., on the feast of Saint Remigius
and at Easter.

Vniuersis presentes litteras inspecturis decanus et capitulum
ecclesie Sancti Marcelli juxta Parisios salutem in Domino. Nouerint
vniuersi nos concessisse, tradidisse et accensauisse ex nunc imperpetuum domino Hemfesto de regno Suecie rectori Fallocopensis et
5 eius heredibus seu ab eo causam habituris vnam masuram sitam
in vico Jocellini sine capite contiguam ex vna parte domui dicti
domini Hemfesti et ex alia parte domui quondem Roberti Blondi
que nunc est fratrum Sancti Maturini ab oppositis domus dicte la
Palmiere in censiua ecclesie nostre pro quinque solidos paris.
10 annui census seu perpetui redditus et oblialis census fundi terre
reddendis et soluendis annuatim de cetero nobis seu ecclesie nostre
a domino Hemfesto uel ab eius causam habentibus duobus terminis
videlicet duobus solidis cum dimidio in festo beati Remigii et oblialis census fundi terre, et duobus solidis cum dimidio ad Pascha
15 sequens contra quam concessionem, tradicionem et accensationem
non venire aliquo jure communi uel speciali per nos uel per alium
set garentizare promittimus contra omnes.
Et si predicto emptori placuerit emere quinque solidos annui
census seu perpetui redditus in terra nostra bene sitos post censum
20 fundi terre placebit nobis hos sumere loco horum. In cuius rei
testimonium eidem domino Hemfredo [1]) presentem litteram magni
nostri sigilli caractere concessimus sigillatam.

---

1) Emphasto (Hemfesto, Hemphasto).

Datum anno Domini millesimo tricentesimo die Dominica post Inuentionem beati Stephani.

Parchment : 240 × 180 mm.
Slit for seal tag. [Seal missing.]
Endorsements : 1) « Littera consensus capituli Sancti Marcelli super alienatione » (Early fourteenth-century hand);
2) « Inventorié XVIII » (Eighteenth-century hand).

XI

1309, February 3, Paris

Paris, Arch. Nat., M 73, n° 10

Deed of the officialis of the Bishop of Paris, in which Guillelmus Bertrandi Canatarius sells 8 sol. 9 den. par. yearly revenue on a house [domus Scarensis] in Clos-Bruneau, to Michael de Sancta-Susanna, tailor, and his wife Johanna for 100 sol. par.

Vniuersis presentes litteras inspecturis officialis curie Parisiensis salutem in Domino. Notum facimus quod in nostra presentia propter hoc personaliter constitutus Guillelmus Bertrandi Canatarius Parisius commorans, asseruit se habere et possidere ac percipere
5 annuatim quatuor terminis Parisius consuetis octo solidos et nouem denarios paris. annui incrementi census seu redditus perpetui, videlicet quinque solidos et decem denarios ex suo proprio conquestu et et [sic] triginta quinque denarios ex suo proprio patrimonio capiendos et leuandos annis singulis super domo que fuit Guillelmi dicti
10 Biterne sita ultra Paruum Pontem Parisius in vico Clausi Brunelli contigua ex vna parte domui Radulphi Scriptoris, et ex altera parte grangie que fuit Gileberti de Volta, sicut se comportat, et extenditur a parte posteriori usque ad ruellam Jocelini Anglici in censiua beate Genouefe Parisius in monte.
15 Quos siquidem octo solidos et nouem denarios annui incrementi census seu perpetui redditus predictus Guillelmus recognouit et confessus fuit coram nobis in jure se vendidisse et nomine pure et simplicis venditionis ex nunc imperpetuum concessisse, derelinquisse et de cetero ac hereditarie dimisisse et quitasse Michaeli de
20 Sancta Susenna talliatori robarum Parisius commoranti et Johanne eius vxori eorumque heredibus ac causam imposterum habituris ab ipsis et quicquid juris, actionis, proprietatis et dominii, possessionis et saisine que uel quas habet et habebat ac habere poterat in predictis quacumque ratione seu causa pro precio centum solidorum
25 jam dicto venditori ab eisdem emptoribus solutorum et traditorum in bona et forti pecunia bene computata et numerata, sicut idem

venditor confessus fuit in jure coram nobis, exceptioni dicte pecunie
non numerate, tradite et solute, renuncians penitus et expresse.

Et promisit dictus venditor per fidem suam in manu nostra prestitam corporalem quod contra predictam venditionem, concessionem, 30
et quitationem per se uel per alium non veniet in futurum immo
predictos octo solidos et nouem denarios paris. annui incrementi
census seu perpetui redditus habendos, leuandos et percipiendos
annuatim dictis terminis super domo a dictis emptoribus et eorum
heredibus ac causam ab eis habituris garantizabit, liberabit et def- 35
fendet in judicio et extra judicium suis sumptibus et expensis ad
usus et consuetudines Francie imposterum contra omnes pro quibus
omnibus et singulis supradictis tenendis et [adim]plendis et de non
veniendo contra ac pro dicta garantizatione facienda et ferenda,
prout superius est [expres]sum prefatus Guillelmus Bertrandi 40
obligauit omnia bona sua et heredum suorum dictis emptoribus
[eorumque] heredibus mobilia et immobilia, presentia et futura,
vbicumque sint et potuerint inueniri [et] ad quoscumque deuenerint
possessores et specialiter in contraplegium quindecim sol. paris.
[annui] incrementi census seu perpetui redditus quos dicebat se 45
habere, possidere et percipere annuatim Parisius super domo Petri
dicti Brifaut bedelli, sita in vico predicto contigua domui predicte,
et renunciauit omnibus exceptionibus tam juris quam facti, deceptionibus circumuentionibus, lesionibus, cauillationibus, fraudibus
et barris que contra premissa possunt obici uel opponi.   50

In cujus rei testimonium sigillum curie Parisiensis presentibus
litteris duximus apponendum ad requisitionem dicti Guillelmi. Datum anno Domini M⁰ CCC⁰ octauo die Lune post festum Purificationis beate Marie Virginis.

                                                        J. de Barra.

Parchment : 210 × 267 mm.
Seal on tag.
Endorsements : 1) « Littera Michaelis de Sancta Susanna »
(Early fourteenth-century hand n⁰ I);
2) « de vendicione census . viij . sol. <cum . ix . den.> » (Early
fourteenth-century hand n⁰ II);
3) « Inventorié XVIII » (Eighteenth-century hand);
4) « 1308 » (Modern hand).

XII

1311, March 31, Paris

Paris, Arch. Nat.,
M 73, n° 13
[12;
also marked 11]

*Deed of the officialis of the Bishop of Paris, in which Michael de
Sancta-Susanna, tailor, and his wife Johanna sell 8 sol. 9 den. par.
yearly revenues on a house [domus Scarensis] in Clos-Bruneau to
Sueno of Sweden, priest-student in Paris, proctor of canon Emphastus [Anfastus] of Skara, for 100 sol. par.*

Vniuersis presentes litteras inspecturis officialis curie Parisiensis salutem in Domino. Notum facimus quod coram nobis propter
hoc personaliter constituti Michael de Sancta-Suzanna scisor pannorum et Johanna eius vxor asseruerunt coram nobis se habere,
5 tenere, et pacifice possidere ex suo proprio conquestu octo solidos
et nouem denarios paris. annui census seu perpetui redditus super
quadam domo que quondam fuit Guillelmi dicti Biterne, sita
Parisius vltra Paruum Pontem in vico Clausi Brunelli, contigua ex
vna parte domui Radulphi Scriptoris, et ex parte altera granchie
10 que fuit de Volta : quos quidem octo solidos et nouem denarios
annui incrementi census seu perpetui redditus predicti Michael et
Johanna recognouerunt et confessi fuerunt coram nobis in jure se
vendidisse et nomine pure et simplicis venditionis ex nunc imperpetuum concessisse, derelinquisse hereditarieque dimisisse et quitauisse
15 domino Suenoni de Swecia presbitero scolari Parisiensi, procuratori domini Anfasti canonici Scarensis, ementi et recipienti nomine
procuratoris ipsius domini Suenoni et pro ipso pro precio et sub
precio centum solidorum paris. iam eisdem emptoribus a dicto
procuratore nomine quo supra traditorum, solutorum et liberatorum
20 in pecunia numerata ante confectionem presencium litterarum.
Et de quibus vocauerunt se dicti venditores plene pro contentis
et bene pagatis cedentes et ex nunc transferentes dicti Michael et
Johanna in dictum procuratorem nomine quo supra ac dominum

152

suum predictum quicquid juris, dominii, possessionis, proprietatis, actionis et saisine habebant et habere poterant et debebant quoquo 25 modo in dictis octo solidis et nouem denariis paris. annui census seu redditus nichil pro se uel suis heredibus in eisdem retinendo et a se penitus abdicando et promiserunt dicti venditores per fidem suam in manu nostra prestitam corporalem quod contra venditionem, traditionem, concessionem, cessionem et translationem predictas 30 per se aut per alium non venient in futurum, immo predictos octo solidos et nouem denarios paris. annui census incrementi seu reddi- tus perpetui habendos, leuandos et percipiendos annuatim quatuor terminis Parisius consuetis a dicto procuratore, nomine quo supra et domino suo predicto eiusque heredibus ac causam ab eis habituris 35 garantizabunt, liberabunt et deffendent in judicio et extra judicium suis sumptibus et expensis ad vsus et consuetudines Francie impos- terum contra omnes pro quibus omnibus et singulis supradictis tenendis et adimplendis et de non veniendo contra ac pro dicta garantizatione facienda et ferenda prout superius est expressum 40 prefati coniuges obligauit dicto procuratori, nomine quo supra ac domino suo predicto obligarunt per fidem suam predictam ac juris- dictioni curie Parisiensis supposuerunt se eorumque quemlibet insolidum et heredes suos ac omnia sua bona, mobilia et immobilia, presentia et futura, vbicumque existencia et potuerint inueniri et ad 45 quoscumque deuenerint possessores, renunciantes insuper dicti ven- ditores per fidem predictam in hoc facto omnibus tam juris quam facti excepcionibus, deceptionibus, circomuentionibus, lesionibus, cauillationibus, barris, fraudibus et aliis quibusque que contra premissa aut aliquod ex eisdem dici possent modo quolibet uel 50 opponi jurique dicenti generalem renunciationem non valere. In cuius rei testimonium sigillum curie Parisiensis duximus litteris presentibus apponendum.

Datum anno Domini M⁰ CCC⁰ decimo, die Mercurii ante Ramos Palmarum.   55

Ansellus.

Parchment : 225 × 280 mm.
Tag for seal. [Seal missing.]
Endorsement : « Littera super censiva [sic] . viij . solidorum et . ix . den. paris. quos consuevit debere domus Scarensis et redempti sunt per procuratorem eiusdem domus » (Early fourteenth-century hand).

153

XIII

1311, April 7 [1]), Paris

Paris, Arch. Nat.,
M 73, n° 12

Livery of seisin of a rent of 8 sol. 9 den. par. given by Robertus, chamberlain of Sainte-Geneviève, to Sueno of Sweden, proctor of canon Emphastus [Anfast] of Skara, on a house [domus Scarensis] in Clos-Bruneau for 100 sol. par.

A touz ceus qui ces lettres verront ffrere Robert, chamberier de Sainte-Geneuieue de Paris, salut. Sachent tuit que, par deuant nous vindrent Michiel de Sainte-Susanne, tailleur de robes et Jehanne sa fame et se dessaisirent en nostre main de huit solz et
5 nuef deniers paris. de cens ou de perpetuel rente que il auoient vendus a monseigneur Suen de Suesce prestre, escolier a Paris, procureur de monseigneur Anfast chanoine de Scaren ou non dudit chanoine et pour lui assis, sus une meson qui fu jadis Guillaume dit Biterne en la rue de Clos Burnel tenant d'une part a Raoul
10 l'Escriuein et d'autre part a la granche qui fu de la Voute c'est a sauoir pour le pris de cent solz paris. si comme il est plus plainement contenu en unes lettres scellees de l'offici[al] de Paris faites sus ce parmi lesquelles ces presentes sont annexiees et nous a la requeste des diz Michiel et Jehanne en saisisimes le dit procureur
15 ou non desus dit et nous en fist de ventes et de saisines ce que il appartient ou puet appartenir en ce cas. Ce fut fait l'an de grace mil trois cens et dis le mesdi [*sic*] [2]) deuant Pasques.

Parchment : 228 × 110 mm.
Tag for seal. [Seal missing.]
No endorsement.

---

1) April 6, if we read *mardi* in the last line of the text, April 7 if we read *mercredi*.
2) *Mesdi* could be *mardi* or *mercredi*.

1322, July 1, Paris
(1321, December 23, Paris)

Paris, Arch. Nat.,
M 73, n° 14 [13]

Vidimus of the officialis of Paris of a letter of Gille Haquin,
provost of Paris, dated December 23, 1321, in which Pelerin de
Compigne sells to Baudet le Flament, burgher of Paris, 37 sol.
par. yearly rent : namely, 25 sol. 4 den. on the house which belonged
to Pierre Briffaut in Clos-Bruneau, and 11 sol. 8 den. on the house
of the « clers escoliers d'Alemaigne », in the censive of Sainte-
Geneviève, for the price of 16 libr. par.

Vniuersis presentes litteras inspecturis officialis curie Parisiensis
salutem in Domino. Notum facimus nos anno Domini millesimo
CCCᵐᵒ vicesimo secundo die Jouis post festum beatorum Petri et
Pauli apostolorum vidisse legisse ac diligenter inspexisse litteras
infrascriptas sigillo prepositure Parisiensis ut prima facie apparebat 5
sigillatas, sanas et integras tenorem de verbo ad verbum qui sequitur continentes.
    A tous ceus qui ces lestres verront Gille Haquin garde de la pre-
voste de Paris salut. Sachet tuit que par deuant nous vint en jugement
Pelerin de Compigne, fils Jehan de Compigne escuier demeurant a 10
Yuri et recongnut en droit lui auoer vendu et par non de pure vente
quitte et octroie a tous jours a Baudet le Flament bourgeois de Paris
a ses hoirs et a tous ceux qui de ly auront cause, trente sept soulz
paris. qu'il auoit et prenoit chacun an a pris fonz de terre aus
quatre termes a Paris a coustumes c'est a sauoir vint et cinc soulz et 15
quatre deniers paris. sur la meson qui fu feu Pierre Briffaut assise a
Paris outre Petit Pont ou clos Burnel [sic] tenant d'une part a Pierre
Felisc et d'autre part a la maeson [sic] qui est aus clers escoliers
d'Alemaigne en la censiue Sainte-Geneuieue du Mont de Paris. Et
onze soulz et huit deniers paris. sur la dite meson des diz clers esco- 20
liers d'Alemaigne tenant d'une part a la dite meson qui fu du dit feu
Pierre Briffaut et d'autre part a la meson aus hoirs feu Pierre le
Flament mouuant partie de la censiue de Sainte-Geneuieue de sus
dite et partie de la censiue Saint-Benoit. Si come il disoit c'est assauoir

25 tout pour le pris de seze liures paris. bone et fort monnoie que le dit
vendeur a ia eue et receue en bons deniers comptent auant la confection
de ces lestres du dit acheteur si come il le confessa et dont il se tint
pour bien paiez par deuant nous et du dit pris il quita et quitte
clama bonnement a touz jours le dit acheteur et ses hoirs. Et promist
30 par son serement fet par deuant nous sur sains evangiles le dit vendeur
que il contre ceste vente la quittance et ottroi dessus diz par aucun
droit quel qu'il soit commun ou especial n'ira ne aler fera a nul jour
par lui ne par autre ainçois la dite vente ni la censive dessus dite
vendue a commencer a prendre a Noel prochain venant au dit ache-
35 teur et a ses hoirs garantira et defendra [...] [1]) envers touz a touz
jours en jugement et hors aus us et aus coustumes de France. Et rendra
le quint denier en non de paiement [...] [2]) vente estoit retraicte ou
eue d'acun en tout ou en partie. Et quant a ce tenir fermement le dit
Pelerin a obligié et souzmis a ses hoirs touz ses biens et de ses hoirs
40 immobles et non immobles presenz et a venir ou qui soient a justice
par le preuost de Paris et par tous autres iustyces pour vendre et
pour desprendre par ces lestres enteriner. Et renunça a ce fait le dit
vendeur et par son serement a touz engins baras, fraudes et deceuan-
ces a action de fait a touz priuileges graces et respiz donnez et a
45 donner et a tout ce qui valoir li paroit en ces cas. En tesmoing de ce
nous auons mis en ces lestres le scel de la preuoste de Paris l'an de
grace mil CCC vint un le mercredi auant Noel.

    Transcriptum autem hujusmodi litterarum fieri fecimus sub
sigillo dicte Parisiensis curie cuiuslibet in omnibus juribus saluo.
50 Datum anno Domini millesimo CCC° XXII° die Jouis post festum
beatorum Petri et Pauli apostolorum supradictis.

G. de P. xvj d.

Parchment : 288 × 230 mm.
Seal on tag.
*Endorsement : 1) « Hec littera dirigit procuratorem domus
Skarensis cui soluet censum .xj. sol. cum .xiij. den., videlicet
Baldeuino Fleming, commoranti in cano [3]) vici Brunelli ex parte
superiori versus orientem » (Fourteenth-century hand n° I);*
*2) « Hic [sic] est littera de censu domus quem emit dominus
Erkallus » (Fourteenth-century hand n° II);*
3) « Inventorié XVII » (Eighteenth-century hand).

---

1) Blurred writing. 2) Blurred writing. 3) *Sic*; probably for *clauso*.

XV

1385, June 19, Paris

Paris, Arch. Nat.,
M 73, n° 15 [14]

Livery of seisin of a rent of 11 sol. 8 den. par. given by Jean Noël, chamberlain of Sainte-Geneviève, to Brynulphus Karlsson [Bryniulphe Charles], provost of the cathedral church of Skara, bought on a house in Clos-Bruneau from Simon l'Alemant, proctor of Perrenelle la Riche, resident in Paris, on the rue Saint-Hilaire, for 12 libr. tur.

A tous ceuls qui ces lettres verront frere Jehan Noel chanoine et chamberier de l'eglise Sainte-Geneuieve de Paris ou Mont salut. Sauoir faisons que l'an de grace mil CCC $\frac{XX}{IIII}$ et cinq le lundi XIXe jour de juing se dessaisy en nostre main Symon l'Alemant ou nom et comme procureur de Perrenelle la Riche femme de feu Estienne 5 le Riche demourant a Paris ou mont Saint-Ylaire des onze sol. et huit den. paris. de crois de cens ou rente annuel et perpetuel que la dicte Perrenelle de son heritage se disoit auoir et prendre chacun an en et sur une maison, court et jardin si comme tout se comporte assis a Paris en la rue de Clos-Brunel plus aplain declerre es lettres 10 de vendue sur ce faites et passes pardevant deux notaires du Chastel-let de Paris parmi lesquelles ces presentes sont annexees, laquelle rente la dicte Perrenelle auoit et a vendue a honnorable home maistre Bryniulphe Charles, preuost en l'eglise cathedrale de Sca-rence, ou royaume de Suece, maistre es ars, escolier estudiant a 15 Paris, pour le pris et la somme de douze liv. tourn. et tout par la fourme et maniere que est contenu es dictes lettres. Et nous requitte le dit Simon ou nom que dessus que d'ycelle rente nous meissions en saisine et possession ledit maistre Bryniulphe lequel par la vertu de ces presentes nous en saississons sauf tous drois le nostre et 20 l'autrui. Et nous tenons a bien paiés des ventes a nous appartenans pour cause de ce.

En tesmoing de ce nous auons mis le seel de la chambre de la

dicte eglise a ces lettres qui furent faites et données l'an et le
25 jour dessus diz.

    Parchment : 290 × 110 mm.
    Tag for seal. [Seal missing.]
    Endorsements : 1) « Inventorié XX » (Eighteenth-century hand) ;
2) « Saisine d'une rente dont étoit chargée la maison de N. Dame
au Clos-Brunel donnée à Brynulphe, chanoine de Scarence en
Suede qui a racheté laditte rente » (Later hand).

XVI

Ca. 1407, Paris

Paris, Arch. Nat.,
M 73, nº 16 [15]

The Statutes of Skara House.

Quoniam lex prodest ut appetitus noxius sub regula limitetur, per quam quilibet, ut honeste viuat, alterum non ledat, jus suum cuique tribuat, informatur, sane scholares in domo Scharensis ecclesie *ad ymaginem Nostre <Domine>* in vico Brunelli commorantes, statuunt infrascripta inter se fideliter obseruanda.   5

Primo statuunt, quod quicumque socio suo uerba obprobriosa, iniuriosa aut contumeliam intulerit, soluat burse vnum francum et iniurias passo satisfaciat secundum dicta sociorum; quod si noluerit, recedat a societate et a domo.

Item statuunt, quod quicumque socium suum inuaserit et ipsum 10 de facto uerberauerit, soluat burse duos francos et secundum enormitatem facti juxta dicta sociorum, satisfaciat leso aut a societate recedat. Et si contingit aliquem aliquo istorum modorum jam dictorum penaliter exire non satisfaciendo burse aut parti lese, volunt quod soluat de anno pro famulo et domo, carebitque toto jure quod 15 in utensilibus et prouisionibus habuit pro tempore factis.

Statuunt 3º, quod quicumque vltra porcionem suam, siue in mensa siue extra, vinum habere voluerit, capiat supra dicam suam et societati secundum conscienciam suam computabit; cujus quidem dice una pars penes famulum, alia penes dominum remaneat, sta- 20 timque recepto vino dicabitur receptum.

Item, quod quis recipit de bursa pro hospitibus suis soluat sicut burse constat.

Item, hora prandii si aliquis extraneus superuenerit, ipse cujus racione dinoscitur venire, si comederit, pro ipso satisfaciat. Si 25 vero non plus racione unius quam alterius quis superuenerit, nulli computabitur.

Item, nullus meretrices infra domum introducat. Quod si fecerit, soluat burse vnum francum, et carebit omni jure quod habuit uel

30 habet in utensilibus et in prouisionibus pro tempore factis, et a
domo recedat, nichilominus pro domo et famulo de anno soluturus.
Item, nullus portam seu hostia nostra iniuriose aut violenter in-
fringat, sibi vinum vel alia usurpando; quicumque fecerit soluat
burse vnum francum, et reparet seu reparare faciat fracta, resti-
35 tuatque ablata; quicumque noluerit, a societate recedat, carendo
omnibus, ut prius, pro domo et famulo nichilominus soluturus.
Quicumque autem casualiter uel uoluntarie fregerit vitra uel alia,
restituat meliora uel saltem eque bona.
Item, nullus verberabit famulum nostrum nec sibi uerba opro-
40 briosa injuste obiciat. Quicumque fecerit, leso satisfaciat et burse
secundum facti exigentiam et sociorum dicta. Qui famulus precipue
seruiat preposito; et nullus mittat extra famulum tempore quo
cibaria habet preparare, nisi alter ad ea respexerit usque ad reditum
suum. Item, si plures concurrunt in rogando ipsum siue mittendo,
45 qui prior est tempore, potior est jure.
Item, nullus in aliquo loco infra portam nisi in latrinis mingat,
uel in potto, ipsum postea ad latrinas deportando, propter malos
fetores euitandos, nec alias immundicias quascumque ibidem ponat.
Quicumque autem fecerit, juxta dicta sociorum emendabit.
50 Item, quicumque in ebdomada per aliquem diem se abstinuerit
uel jejunauerit, tota societate non tamen jejunante, reddantur sibi
pecunie pro isto die, et sibimet prouidebit.
Item, nullus se intromittat de lignis, singulariter ad suam ca-
meram portando, aut alia quouis modo ad proprium vsum appli-
55 cando, sed maneant pro bono communi, videlicet preparando cibaria
uel, omnibus simul existentibus et volentibus, in aula comburendo.
Item, singuli componant pro prouisionibus faciendis in vino,
lignis et aliis necessariis. Et si contingat aliquem sociorum recedere
ante earum consumptionem, non delicti causa in domo commissa,
60 si fuerit in vino et ante apercionem ejus, socii remanentes reddant
sibi portionem suam in pecunia quanta sibi competere potest. Si
autem post apercionem ejus recesserit, ut premittitur, et vinum
notabiliter pejoratum sentitur, soluatur sibi minus, secundum
judicium duorum in tali materia expertorum. Residue vero proui-
65 siones et vtensilia, que ipsum contingere possunt, sibi restituantur.
Item, si durante ista societate jam contracta, Deus aliquem reuoca-
verit ab hac vita, socii superuiuentes sibi subueniant honorifice, ejus
corpus tradentes sepulture, assistentiam omnem quam valent impen-
dendo. Etiam quilibet de superuiuentibus tres vigilias, tot psalmos
70 penitentiales pro anima defuncti legat, et tres missas celebrabit aut

160

celebrari procuret infra lapsum trium ebdomadarum a die obitus computandarum. Illis ebdomadis tribus elapsis, quicumque hoc non fecerit, ab esu carnium, vsque dum totaliter compleuerit, abstinebit.

Et ego Siggo Odonis, predicte domus procurator, propria manu me subscribo, volens et sub bona fide promittens me omnia et 75 singula suprascripta inuiolabiliter obersuare.

Et ego Gunno Andree propria manu me subscribo, volens et sub bona fide promittens me omnia et singula suprascripta inuiolabiliter obseruare.

Et ego Henninghus Rocstede propria manu me subscripsi, volens 80 et sub fide bona promittens me singula suprascripta inuiolabiliter obseruare.

Et ego Henricus Eueraerdi de Yselstein propria manu me subscribo, volens et sub bona fide promittens me singula supradicta inviolabiliter obseruare.   85

Parchment : 284 × 192 mm.
Not sealed.
Endorsements : 1) « Statutum sodalitatis domus Scarensis Ecclesiae quae est ad insigne Dominae Nostrae in Clauso Brunelli »
(Eighteenth-century hand n⁰ I) ;
2) « Inventorié XVIII » (Eighteenth-century hand n⁰ II) ;
3) « Inventorié XLIX » (Eighteenth-century hand n⁰ III).
Edited : Auctarium II, Introd., pp. xi-xii.

XVII

1486, April 27, Paris   Paris, Arch. Nat.,
                                                   M 73, n⁰ 17 [16]

*Receipt given by Robert du Sauchoy, proctor of the canons of
Saint-Benoît-Bien-Tourné, to Pierre Cesaris [Wagner], receptor of
the English-German Nation of the University of Paris, for 12 sol.
par. paid by the Nation on « l'hotel de Suesse » [domus Scaren-
sis] « pour le cens ou fons de terre ».*

    Receu par moy Robert du Sauchoy prestre, procureur et rece-
veur de messeigneurs les chanoines et chappitre de Saint-Benoist
le Bien Tourné a Paris de la Nacion d'Alemaigne par les mains de
maistre Pierre Cesaris receueur de laditte Nacion la somme de
5 douze sol. paris. que laditte nacion deuoit aus dits seigneurs par
composicion et appoinctement fait entre eulx pour raison et a
cause d'une maison seant en la Rue du cloz Bruneau nomme l'ostel
de Suesse ou quel est l'Ymaige Notre Dame sur lequel mes dits
seigneurs ont droit de prendre chacun an au jour saint Remy pour
10 le cens ou fons de terre la somme de deux sol. . x . den. obol.
paris. Pour laquelle somme de . xij . sol. paris. messeigneurs ont
quitté laditte nacion tant pour les arrerages qui en pouoient estre
d'eulx de tout le temps passé jusques au jour de saint Remy der-
nier passe qui fut $\overset{\text{C}}{\text{IIII}}$ $\overset{\text{XX}}{\text{IIII}}$ et cinq comme aussi pour les depenses
15 fais en certaine cause en Chastellet de Paris entre laditte nacion et
messeigneurs sus dits a cause des dits deulx sol. . x . den. obol.
paris. de fons de terre dont laditte maison est redeuable ausdits
seigneurs et desquelz . ij . sol. . x . den. obol. paris. laditte nacion
en doit passer congnoissance ausdits seigneurs par deuant deux
20 notaires par ledit appoinctement ainsi fait et accordé entre lesdits
seigneurs et laditte nacion.
    Et en ce faisant, Je Robert dessus nommé en quitte et prometz
acquiter laditte nacion envers messeigneurs susdits.

Tesmoing mon saing manuel cy mis ce XXVIIe jour du mois
Avril mil $\overset{\text{C}}{\text{IIII}}$ $\overset{\text{XX}}{\text{IIII}}$ et six.   25

R. du Sauchoy.
[s. m.]

Paper : 214 × 143 mm.
Not sealed.
Endorsement : « Sexdecim anni sunt quod apunctuamentum istud
est factum » (Fifteenth-century hand).
N°s XVII - XVIII [vielle cote : 16 - 17] documents are tied
together.

XVIII

1502, December 31, Paris

Paris, Arch. Nat.,
M 73, n° 17

Receipt given by Guillaume Malicorne, former canon of Saint-Benoît-Bien-Tourné, to Pierre Cesaris [Wagner], dean of the English-German Nation, for 13 sol. 11 den. ob. paris., amount paid by the Nation for five years of arrears on the house Image de Notre-Dame [Skara House].

Receu par moy Guillaume Malicorne chanoine de Saint Merry a Paris et parauant chanoine de l'eglise monseigneur Saint Benoist le Bien Tourné a Paris, de messeigneurs de la nacion d'Almaigne par les mains de maistre Pierre Cesar doyen de ladicte nacion la

5 somme de treize sols unze deniers obol. paris. pour cinq années d'arrerages escheues au terme de Saint Remy l'an mil cinq cent pour lesquelles années j'ay este recu de ladicte eglise a cause de fons de terre de leur maison assise en la Rue du Cloux Bruneau ou pend l'Imaige Nostre Dame. De laquelle somme de . xiii . sol. . xj .

10 obol. paris. je les tient quictes et prometz acquiter.

Tesmoing mon seing manuel cy mis le derrenier jour de decembre l'an mil cinq cent et deux.

G. Malicornensis.

Paper : 198 × 106 mm.
Not sealed.
Endorsements : 1) « Quitancia Sancti-Benedicti » (Early sixteenth-century hand n° I);
2) on a leaflet, attached to the receipt : « Quitancie Sancti Benedicti pro domo Scarensi Nacionis Alamanie » (Sixteenth-century hand n° II).

MANUSCRIPTS
AND
ARCHIVES MATERIAL

MANUSCRIPTS AND ARCHIVES MATERIAL

P a r i s

   a. Archives Nationales :
     H 2587; H 2588.
     M 73 n°s 1-12; 13 [12, also 11]; 14 [13]; 15 [14];
     16 [15]; 17 [16]; 17 repeated.
     N I Seine 4 and 35; N II Seine 32; N IV Seine 4, 10,
     and 64.
     S 1626^1 - S 1626^4; S 1630^6; S 1631^8; S 1632; S 1633.

   b. Archives de la Sorbonne :
     Reg. 91 (85) ; Carton 14 (17).

   c. Bibliothèque de l'Arsenal :
     Ms. 1228.

   d. Bibliothèque Nationale :
     Latin 16070.
     Nouvelle acquisition lat. 535.

   e. Bibliothèque Sainte-Geneviève :
     Ms. 369 (E. f. in fol. 11).

S t o c k h o l m

   Riksarkivet :
     Dipl. n° 229.
     Seals :
       a. Riksarkivet *D. S.* [*Diplomatarium Suecanum*] 714;
         764; 1075; 2236; 2279; 3494.

       b. S. D. [*Svenskt Diplomatarium,* referred to in my
         text as *D. S. n. s.* (*Diplomatarium Suecanum,* new
         series)] 227; 649; 1626.

       c. R. A. P. [Riksarkivet perg.] seals of the city of
         Falköping, 1441, and of Siggo Uddsson, 1434
         (otherwise not marked).

U p s a l a

   Universitetsbibliotek :
     Seal of the city of Växjö, 1489.

RESUMES IN FRENCH
AND SWEDISH

RESUME FRANÇAIS

Les cent cinquante ans de l'histoire de la Maison de Skara (1292-1435) montrent clairement que les évêques de Skara s'intéressèrent profondément à cet hospice pour étudiants suédois à l'Université de Paris. La maison fut achetée en 1292 par Emphastus, chanoine de Växjö et ensuite de Skara, durant l'épiscopat de Brynulphus Algotsson (1278-1317), qui avait étudié de nombreuses années à Paris. Un autre illustre étudiant de la Maison, Brynulphus Karlsson, y vécut en tant que procureur et continue de s'y intéresser durant son épiscopat (1405-1424). Siggo Uddsson, qui y réforma la discipline et la vie liturgique, pourvut de statuts (vers 1407) la Communauté des clercs qui vivaient en ces murs et termina aussi sa carrière comme évêque de Skara.

La Maison de Skara était située à l'est de la Rue Clos-Bruneau, qui devint plus tard la Rue « Saint »-Jean-de-Beauvais (aujourd'hui, Jean-de-Beauvais). A l'arrière, elle tenait à une impasse, la Rue Josselin, appelée par la suite Bouvard. Les documents de la fin du quatorzième siècle précisent mieux son emplacement, la situant entre l'Ecole de Droit Canon, appelée Le Grand Décret, et la Rue Saint-Hilaire.

Les textes relatifs à l'histoire de la Maison de Skara révèlent un nombre de personnes jusqu'ici inconnues, qui habitaient et étaient propriétaires de maisons dans le Clos-Bruneau, des environs de 1285 jusqu'aux environs de 1299 : Guillebertus de Volta; Guillelmus Biterne, bedeau de la Nation Française et son épouse Johanna; son gendre Guillelmus de Orvalle et sa femme Thomassia; Petrus Roulle, bedeau; Conradus, enlumineur; Robertus le Coustepointier et son épouse Johanna; Richardus, bedeau; Thomas Barsail; Guillelmus Calot Burgundus; Maître Robertus Blondi; Radulphus Scriptor; frère Jacobus de Duaco, Mathurin; de 1300 à 1322 : Pierre Briffaut, bedeau; Pierre Felisc.

Ils nous renseignent sur les personnes qui percevaient des revenus sur des biens sis au Clos-Bruneau entre 1285 et 1299 : Johannes de Volta; le chanoine Richardus Tesson; Philippus Carpentarius et sa femme Alipdis; Maître Arnandus Provincialis; Johannes de Campis, bourgeois; Arnulphus as Maillez; Guillelmus Bertrandi Canatarius; Guiardus de Latigniaco, bourgeois, et Johanna de Archiis, sa femme; Maître Arnaldus de Ambella et Nicolaa, son épouse. Entre 1300 et 1322 : Michael de Sancta-Susanna et sa femme Johanna; Pelerin de Compigne; Baudet le Flament; vers 1385 : Perrenelle la Riche, femme d'Estienne le Riche.

La maison achetée par Emphastus, « deux corps et logis » ou « deux corps d'ostel » (deux constructions d'une seule façade), fut plus tard appelée *domus Scarensis* ou Hôtel Suesse. Après 1392, une partie de la Maison de Skara fut identifiée par l'enseigne « Ymage de Notre Dame ». L'autre partie, qui n'eut pas d'enseigne au quinzième siècle, fut appelée Maison du Cadran avant le milieu du seizième. La Maison de Skara (Maison Notre Dame et Maison du Cadran) était adjacente à deux autres propriétés de la Nation Anglo-Allemande, les Petites Ecoles de Décret et la Maison de Saint-Michel ou Petit-Aigle. La Maison Notre Dame garda son nom jusqu'au milieu du dix-huitième siècle où l'on perd sa trace.

L'emplacement approximatif actuel serait entre les angles sud-est et nord-est formés par l'intersection des Rues Jean-de-Beauvais et des-Ecoles, à l'est de la petite place Marcelin-Berthelot, devant le Collège de France.

La maison d'Emphastus, donnée plus tard au chapitre de Skara, survécut à quatre cents années d'adversités et demeura une source à la fois de soucis et de revenus pour la Nation. Après le premier quart du quinzième siècle, elle perdit son caractère d'hospice ou de collège pour les étudiants suédois, mais conserva sur sa façade l'image de la sainte patronne de la Cathédrale de Skara, Notre Dame.

SVENSK RESUME

Skara Husets hundrafemtioåriga historia (1292-1435) visar tydligt att Skara biskopar var djupt intresserade av detta härbärge för svenska studenter, som studerade vid Paris Universitet. Hemphastus köpte huset (1292) under Brynulphi biskopsämbete 1278-1317 som själv var student i Paris i många år. Brynulphus Karlsson bodde i Skara Huset som dess procurator och behöll sitt intresse för huset under sitt episkopat (1405-1427).

Reformatorn av disciplin och liturgiskt liv i Skara Huset, Siggo Uddsson, författare till STATUTES (omkring 1407) för lärjungesamfundet i Skara Huset, avslutade sin karriär som biskop i Skara (1424-1435).

Skara Huset var beläget på östra sidan av Rue Clos Bruneau, som senare blev Rue « Saint »-Jean-de-Beauvais (numera Jean-de-Beauvais). Bakom huset löpte återvändsgränden Rue Josselin, senare kallad Bouvard. Mot slutet av trettonhundratalet beskrevs platsen mer precist att ligga mellan skolan för kanonisk rätt som kallades Grand Décret, och Rue Saint Hilaire.

Dokumenten, rörande Skara Husets historia, avslöjar ett antal hittills okända invånare och ägare av husen i Clos Bruneau från omkring 1285 till omkring 1299 : Guillebertus de Volta; Guillelmus Biterne, pedell i Franska Nationen, och hans hustru Johanna, hans måg Guillelmus de Orvalle och dennes hustru Thomassia; Petrus Roulle, pedell; Conradus, illuminator; Robertus le Coustepointier och hans hustru Johanna; Richardus, pedell; Thomas Barsail; Guillelmus Calot Burgundus; Mäster Robertus Blondi; Radulphus Scriptor; frater Jacobus de Duaco Mathurin; från 1300-1322 Pierre Felisco.

Handlingarna ger upplysningar om personer, som erhållit inkomster från egendomarna i Clos Bruneau mellan 1285-1299 : Johanna de Volta; domkyrkopräst Richardus Tesson; Phillipus Carpentarius och hans hustru Alipdis; Mäster Arnandus Provincialis; Johannes de Campis, borgare; Arnulphus as Maillez; Guillelmus Bertrandi Canatarius; Guiardus de Latigniaco, borgare, och Johanna de Archiis, hans hustru; Mäster Arnaldus de Ambella och Nicolaa, hans maka. Mellan 1300-1322 : Michael de Sancta Susanna och hans hustru Johanna; Pelerin de Compigne; Baudet le Flament; omkring 1385 : Perrenelle la Riche, hustru till Estienne le Riche.

Det hus som Hemphastus köpt (två byggnader, som såg ut som en) kallades senare *domus Scarensis*, Hôtel Suesse. Efter 1392 identifierades ena delen av Skara Huset med en skylt av « Ymage de Notre Dame » (Madonnabilden). Den andra delen, som under fjortonhundratalet ej hade någon skylt, kallades mot mitten av femtonhundratalet, Maison de Cadran. Skara Huset (Notre Dame och Maison de Cadran) var grannhus till två andra byggnader, som tillhörde Engelsk-Tyska Nationen, Petites Ecoles de Décret och Saint-Michel eller Petit-Aigle-Huset.

Huset Notre Dame behöll sitt namn till mitten av sjuttonhundratalet, då vi förlorar spåret av det. Den ungefärliga platsen för det idag torde vara mellan de östra hörnen av Rue Jean-de-Beauvais och Rue des-Ecoles.

Det hus som tillhörde Hemphastus, domkyrkopräst i Växjö, donerades senare till Skara domkapitel, överlevde fyra hundra år av motgångar och blev en källa av både oro och inkomst för nationen. Efter 1425 förlorade det karaktären av härbärge eller college för svenska studenter, men behöll på sin fasad bilden av Skara Domkyrkas skyddshelgon, Vår Fru (Madonnan), Notre Dame.

BIBLIOGRAPHY

ANNERSTEDT, C., ed., *Scriptores Rerum Svecicarum Medii Aevi,* III, Upsaliae, 1871; 1876.

ANNERSTEDT, C., ed., *Upsala Universitets Historia,* v. I (1477-1654), Upsala, [1877].

BÅÅTH, L. M., ed., *Diplomatarium Svecanum. Appendix. Acta Pontificum Svecica,* I. *Acta Cameralia.* Vol. I. *Ann. 1062-1370;* vol. II. *Ann. 1371-1492,* Holmiae, 1936-1942; 1957.

BECKMANN, J. H., ed., *Johannes Kerer, Statuta Collegii Sapientiae. The Statutes of the Collegium Sapientiae in Freiburg University. Freiburg, Breisgau, 1497,* Lindau & Konstanz, 1957.

BEICHNER, P. E., « Daun Piers, Monk and Business Administrator », *Speculum,* 34 (1959), 611-619.

BERG, H., - I. SVALENIUS, *Växjö stads historia, tiden fram till 1718,* Växjö, 1956.

BERTY, A., - L. M. TISSERAND, - C. PLATON, *Topographie historique du vieux Paris,* v. [VI] *Région centrale de l'Université* (Histoire générale de Paris; collection de documents publiée sous les auspices de l'édilité parisienne), Paris, 1897.

Bibliotheca Hagiographica Latina Antiquae et Mediae aetatis, Bruxelles, T. I (1898-1899) ; T. II (1900-1901).

BOËTHIUS, G., - A. L. ROMDAHL, *Uppsala domkyrka 1285-1435,* Uppsala, 1935.

BOYCE, G. C., *The English-German Nation in the University of Paris during the Middle Ages,* Bruges, 1927.

BRILIOTH, Y., *Svenska Kyrkans Historia* (ed. H. Holmquist - H. Pleijel), II. *Den senare medeltiden 1274-1521*, Stockholm-Uppsala, 1941.

BUDINSZKY, A., *Die Universität Paris und die Fremden an derselben im Mittelalter. Ein Beitrag zur Geschichte dieser hohen Schule*, Berlin, 1876.

BULAEUS [DU BOULAY], C. E., *Historia Universitatis Parisiensis*, V, Paris, 1670.

CARLSSON, G., « Paris-Uppsala. Ett stycke tidig svensk universitetshistoria », *Kyrkohistorisk Årsskrift*, 55 (1955), 229-238.

CARLSSON, G., *Sveriges historia till våra dagar* (eds. E. Hildebrand - L. Stavenow), v. 3. *Senare medeltiden, 1. Tidsskedet 1389-1448*, Stockholm, 1941.

CHATELAIN, E., « Inventaire des Archives de la Nation d'Allemagne en 1721 », *Revue des bibliothèques*, 1 (1891), 65-76.

CHATELAIN, E., « Le „ Livre ” ou „ Cartulaire ” de la Nation d'Angleterre et d'Allemagne dans l'ancienne université de Paris », *Mémoires de la Société de l'Histoire de Paris*, 18 (1891), 73-100.

CHEVALIER, [C.] U. [J.], *Repertorium hymnologicum. Catalogue des chants, hymnes, proses, séquences, tropes en usage dans l'Église Latine depuis les origines jusqu'à nos jours*, Louvain, I-VI, 1892-1921.

CLAUDIN, A., *Liste chronologique des imprimeurs parisiens du quinzième siècle, 1470-1500*, Paris, 1901.

DAAE, L., *Matrikler over Nordiske Studerende ved fremmede Universiteter*, Christiana, 1885.

[DAHLBERG, E. J.], *Suecia antiqua et hodierna*, I-IV, Holmiae, [1667-1716].

DENIFLE, H. - AE. CHATELAIN, ed., *Chartularium Universitatis Parisiensis*, I-IV, Paris, 1889-1897.

DENIFLE, H. - AE. CHATELAIN, ed., *Liber Procuratorum Nationis Anglicanae (Alemanniae) in Universitate Parisiensi* (Auctarium Chartularii Universitatis Parisiensis, I-II), Paris, 1937 (editio nova).

176

DU BREUL, J., *Le Théatre des antiquitez de Paris où est traictê de la fondation des Eglises et Chapelles de la Cité, Université, Ville, et Diocèse de Paris : comme aussi de l'institution du Parlement, fondation de l'Université et Collèges, et autres choses remarquables. Divisé en quatre livres*, Paris, 1612.

ENGELSTOFT, P., - S. DAHL, *Dansk Biografisk Leksikon*, vol. X, København, 1936.

ENGELSTOFT, P., « Noget om Fremmedes Studeringer i Paris i 12 og 13 Aarhundrede », *Skandinavisk Museum*, 5 (1802), [5e part] 54-94.

ERSLEV, KR., - W. CHRISTENSEN, - A. HUDE, *Danmarks Breve fra Middelalderen* (Repertorium Diplomaticum Regni Danici Mediaevalis), v. I *(1085-1350)*; v. II *(1351-1400)*; v. III *(1401-1450)*; v. IV *(Arkivoversigt, Registre)*, København, 1894-1912.

EUBEL, C., *Hierarchia Catholica Medii Aevi*, I-II, Münster, 1913-1914.

FANT, G. F., *Antiquitates Academiae Upsaliensis Dissertatio... sub moderamine Mag. Erici M. Fant*, Upsaliae, 1789.

FANT, E. M., ed., *Scriptores rerum Svecicarum Medii Aevi ex schedis praecipue Nordinianis collectos dispositos ac emendatos*, Upsaliae, 1818, I.

FÉLIBIEN, M. - G. LOBINEAU, *Histoire de la ville de Paris*, Paris, 1725, v. 2, pt. 1 [IV].

FISCHER, E., *Västergötlands kyrkliga konst under medeltiden* (Västergötland A : 2. Bidrag till landskapets kulturhistoria och naturbeskrivning), Uppsala, 1920.

FRANKLIN, A., *Les anciens plans de Paris, Notices historiques et topographiques*, I-II, Paris, 1878-1880.

GABRIEL, A. L., « Robert de Sorbonne », *Revue de l'Université d'Ottawa*, 23 (1953), 473-514.

GALLÉN, J., *La Province de Dacie de l'Ordre des Frères Prêcheurs*, vol. I : *Histoire générale jusqu'au Grand Schisme*, Helsingfors, 1946.

177

GANDILHON, R., *Sigillographie des universités de France*, Paris, [1952].

GEFFROY, A., « Les étudiants suédois à Paris, au quatorzième siècle », *Revue des Sociétés savantes*, 5 (1858), 659-669.

GÉRAUD, H., *Paris sous Philippe-le-Bel, d'après des documents originaux et notamment d'après un manuscrit contenant le rôle de la taille imposée sur les habitants de Paris l'an 1292* (Collection de Documents inédits sur l'Histoire de France), Paris, 1837.

GILSON, E., *History of Christian Philosophy in the Middle Ages*, New York, 1955.

GLORIEUX, P., *Les origines du Collège de Sorbonne* (Texts and Studies in the History of Mediaeval Education, n⁰ 8, ed. A. L. Gabriel - J. N. Garvin), Notre Dame, Indiana, 1959.

GUÉRARD, M., ed., *Cartulaire de l'Eglise Notre-Dame de Paris* (Collection des cartulaires de France, IV-VII. Collection de Documents inédits sur l'Histoire de France), Paris, 1850.

GUESNON, A., « Un collège inconnu des Bons Enfants d'Arras à Paris du XIIIe au XVe siècle », *Mémoires de la Société Historique de Paris*, 42 (1915), 1-37.

HÉBERT, M., - J. THIRION, - S. OLIVIER, *Catalogue général des cartes, plans et dessins d'architecture*. Tome premier, *Série N*. (Ministère de l'Education Nationale. Direction des Archives de France), Paris, 1958.

HILDEBRAND, H., *Skara domkyrka. Minnesskrift till den restaurerade domkyrkans invigning den 26 oktober 1894*, Stockholm, 1894.

HILLAIRET, J., *Évocation du vieux Paris*, Paris, 1952, I-II.

HOFFBAUER, F., ed., *Paris à travers les âges : aspects successifs des monuments et quartiers historiques de Paris depuis le XIIIe siècle jusqu'à nos jours fidèlement restitués d'après les documents authentiques*, Paris, 1885, I-II.

HOFMEISTER, A., ed., *Die Matrikel der Universität Rostock*, vol. I *(Mich. 1419 - Mich. 1499)*, Rostock, 1889.

HOLMA, H., - A. MALINIEMI, *Les étudiants finlandais à Paris au moyen âge*, Helsinki, 1937.

HUGNIN, AL. FR., *Plan détaillé du Quartier de Ste-Geneviève. Levé géometriquement par Feu M. l'abbé de La Grive Géographe de la ville de Paris*, Paris, 1757.

JAILLOT, J. B. M., *Recherches critiques, historiques et topographiques sur la ville de Paris, depuis ses commencements connus jusqu'à présent; avec le Plan de chaque Quartier*, IV-V, Paris, 1782.

JESSEN, F. v., ed., *Danske i Paris Gennem Tiderne udgivet af Association Franco-Danoise i Paris*, v. I-II, København, 1936-1938.

JOHANSSON, H., *Hemsjömanualet, en liturgi-historisk studie* (Acta Historico-Ecclesiastica Suecana, H. Pleijel ed., Lund, 24), Stockholm-Lund, 1950.

JOHNSEN, A. O., « Les relations intellectuelles entre la France et la Norvège (1150-1214) », *Le Moyen Age*, 57 (1951), 247-268.

JØRGENSEN, E., « Nogle Bemaerkninger om danske studerende ved Tysklands Universiteter i Middelalderen », *Historisk Tidsskrift* [8] Raekke, 6 (1916), 197-214.

JØRGENSEN, E., « Nordiske Studierejser i Middelalderen. Nordboerne ved Universitetet i Paris fra det 13. Aarhundredes Begyndelse til det 15. Aarhundredes Midte », *Historisk Tidsskrift* [8] Raekke, 5 (1915), 331-382.

KARLSSON, K. H., « Electus Björn i Skara samt Striderna om domprosteriet i Skara 1449-1475 », *Kyrkohistorisk Årsskrift*, 6 (1905), 27-31.

KARLSSON, K. H., ed., *Svenskt Diplomatarium, Supplement* [*1401-1420*], IV, Stockholm, 1903-1904.

KELLERMAN, G., « Från medeltid till reformation. Kyrkliga förhållanden under den utgående medeltiden », *Kyrkohistorisk Årsskrift*, 33 (1933), 1-104.

KEUSSEN, H., *Die Matrikel der Universität Köln* (Publikationen der Gesellschaft für Rheinische Geschichtskunde nᵒ 8), vol. I *(1389-1475)*, Bonn, 1928; vol. II *(1476-1559)*, Bonn, 1919; vol. III *(Nachträge 1389-1559 und Register)*, Bonn, 1931.

KIBRE, P., *The Nations in the Mediaeval Universities* (Mediaeval Academy of America, Publication nᵒ 49), Cambridge, Mass., 1948.

KOHLER, CH., *Catalogue des manuscrits de la Bibliothèque Sainte-Geneviève*, I-II, Paris, 1893-1896.

179

KUMLIEN, K., « Svenskarna vid utländska universitet under medeltiden », *Historiska Studier tillägnade Sven Tunberg den 1 Februari 1942*, Uppsala, 1942, 143-169.

LANGEBEK, J., - P. F. SUHM, ed., *Scriptores rerum Danicarum Medii Aevi*, Hauniae, T. VI-VII, 1786-1792.

LEBEUF, J., *Histoire de la ville et de tout le diocèse de Paris*, I-VI, Paris, 1883-93.

Lexikon für Theologie und Kirche, IX, Freiburg im Br., 1937.

LILJEGREN, J. G., ed., *Svenskt Diplomatarium. Diplomatarium Suecanum*, v. I *(817-1285)*, Stockholm, 1829.

LUNDHOLM, K. G., « Vinstorpaätten och släkter med denna ätts vapen », *Äldre Svenska Frälsesläkter*, I (1957), 95-105.

MAURY, L., « Les Étudiants scandinaves à Paris (XIe - XVe siècles) », *Annales de l'Université de Paris*, 9 (1934), 223-246.

MICHAËLSSON, K., *Études sur les noms de personne français d'après les rôles de taille parisiens (rôles de 1292, 1296-1300, 1313)*, (Uppsala Universitets Årsskrift), I *(Thèse)*, Uppsala [1927]; II *(Lexique raisonné des noms de baptême, A-B)*, Uppsala, 1936.

MICHAËLSSON, K., *Le livre de la taille de Paris l'an 1296* (Romanica Gothoburgensia n° 7), Göteborg, 1958.

MICHANEK, G., ed., *Skalder i Skara en antologi... med illustrationer av Stig Trägårdh*, Stockholm, [1952].

MOLINIER, A., ed., [sous la direction et avec une Préface de M. A. Longnon], *Obituaires de la province de Sens.* Tome I *(Diocèses de Sens et de Paris)*, pt. 1-2 (Recueil des Historiens de la France. Obituaires), Paris, 1902.

Monumenta historica Universitatis Carolo-Ferdinandeae Pragensis. Tomus I. *Liber Decanorum Facultatis Philosophicae Universitatis Pragensis ab anno Christi 1367, usque ad annum 1585*, Pars I-II, Prague, 1830; 1832. — Tomus II, Pars I [II] *Album seu Matricula Facultatis juridicae Universitatis Pragensis ab anno Christi 1372, usque ad annum 1418*, Prague, 1834. — *Monumenta historica Universitatis Pragensis.* Tomus III. *Statuta Universitatis Pragensis*, ed. A. Dittrich - A. Spirk, Prague, [1848 ?].

180

MUSSET, L., *Les peuples scandinaves au moyen âge*, Paris, 1951.

NYGREN, E., « Ericus Olais och andra svenskars studiebesök i Siena, » *Kyrkohistorisk Årsskrift*, 19 (1918), 118-126.

NYLANDER, I., *Das Kirchliche Benefizialwesen Schwedens während des Mittelalters. Die Periode der Landschaftsrechte* (Rättshistoriskt Bibliotek. Ser. I.), Stockholm-Lund, 1953.

OLDE, E. M., *De Universitate Parisiensi a Svecis Medio Aevo frequentata. Dissertatio preside Joh. Henr. Schröder*, Upsaliae, 1830.

OMONT, H., « Nouvelles acquisitions du Département des Manuscrits de la Bibliothèque Nationale », *Bibliothèque de l'École des Chartes*, 53 (1892), 333-382.

PERDRIZET, P., *Le calendrier de la nation d'Allemagne de l'ancienne Université de Paris* (Publications de la Faculté des Lettres de l'Université de Strasbourg, n° 79), Paris, 1937.

PERINGSKIÖLD, J., *Monumenta Ullerakerensia cum Upsalia nova illvstrata*, Stockholm, 1719.

RITTER, G., *Die Heidelberger Universität. Ein Stück deutscher Geschichte. Erster Band. Das Mittelalter (1386-1508)*, Heidelberg, 1936.

ROMDAHL, A. L., - S. DAHLGREN, *Skara domkyrkas byggnadshistoria* (Västergötland B : 5. Bidrag till landskapets kulturhistoria och naturbeskrivning), Uppsala, 1928.

RYDELL, CH., *Skara, Urbs Gothorum vetustissima; Quam, Consentiente Amplissima Facultate Philosophica, Sub Praesidio Admod. Reverendi atq; Celeberrimi viri Dn. Joannis Steuchii,... dissertatione graduali... submittit... Christophorus Rydell*, Upsaliae, 1719.

SÄLLSTRÖM, Å. M., *Aristokrati och hierarki i det medeltida Sverige. I. Studier kring Kalmarmötet år 1397*, Lund - Malmö, 1951.

SÄLLSTRÖM, Å. M., « Nordiska delegater till Konstanz », *Technica & Humaniora. Festskrift till Anders Nevsten 18 mars 1950*, Malmö, 1951, pp. 101-112.

SAMARAN, CH., - AE. A. VAN MOÉ, ed., *Liber procuratorum Nationis Anglicanae (Alemanniae) in Universitate Parisiensi* (Auctarium Chartularii Universitatis Parisiensis III), Paris, 1935.

SANDBERG, E., *Skara stads äldre gator och torg*, Skara, [1948].

SAUVAL, H., *Histoire et recherches des antiquités de la ville de Paris*, I-III, Paris, 1733.

SCHMID, T., « Trois légendes de saint Sigfrid », *Analecta Bollandiana*, 60 (1942), 82-90.

SCHÜCK, H., « Svenska Pariserstudier under medeltiden », *Kyrkohistorisk Årsskrift*, 1 (1900), 9-78.

SCHÜCK, H., *Ecclesia Lincopensis. Studier om Linköpingskyrkan under medeltiden och Gustav Vasa* (Acta Universitatis Stockholmiensis. Stockholm Studies in History nº 4), Stockholm, 1959.

Scriptores rerum Danicarum Medii Aevi, Tom. I-III, J. Langebek, ed., Hafniae, 1772-1774; Tom. IV-VII, J. Langebek - P. F. Suhm, ed., Hauniae, 1776-1792; Tom. VIII, J. Langebek - P. F. Suhmius - L. Engelstoft - E. C. Werlauff, ed., Hauniae, 1834; Tom. IX, J. Langebek - Legati Hjelmstjerne - Rosencroniani Curatores, ed., Hauniae, 1878.

Scriptores rerum Svecicarum Medii Aevi, Tom. I. E. M. Fant, ed., Upsaliae, 1818; Tom. II. E. G. Geijer et J. H. Schröder, ed., Upsaliae, 1828; Tom. III. C. Annerstedt. ed., Upsaliae, 1871, 1876.

SILFVERSTOLPE, C., ed., *Svenskt Diplomatarium*, I *(1401-1407)*; II *(1408-1414)*; III *(1415-1420)*; Stockholm, 1875-1884; 1879-1887; 1885-1902.

SJÖDIN, L., « Gustav Vasas Barndoms — och Ungdomstid », *Historiska Studier tillägnade Sven Tunberg den 1 Februari 1942*, Uppsala, 1942, 225-261.

SÖDERBERG, B., *Medeltida kyrkokonst. Skara stift i ord och bild*, Stockholm, 1949.

STOCK, F., *Die ersten deutschen Buchdrucker in Paris um 1500* (Volksdeutsche Quellen und Darstellungen nº 1), Freiburg in Br., 1940.

SWENSSON, H., *Skara i bild av Birgitta Flink*. Stockholm, 1952.

THÖRNQVIST, C., « Nordiska studenter i Prag efter 1409 », *Kyrkohistorisk Årsskrift*, 30 (1930), 139-141.

THUROT, CH., *De l'organisation de l'enseignement dans l'Université de Paris, au Moyen Age. Thèse présenteé à la faculté des Lettres de Paris*, Paris-Besançon, 1850.

TOULOUSE, M., *La Nation Anglaise-Allemande de l'Université de Paris des origines à la fin du XVᵉ siècle*, Paris, 1939.

VALLÉE, L., *Catalogue des plans de Paris et des cartes de l'Ile de France, de la Généralité, de l'Élection, de l'Archevêché, de la Vicomté, de l'Université, du Grenier à Sel et de la cour des Aydes de Paris conservés à la section des Cartes et Plans*, Paris, 1908.

VALOUS, [G.] de, - SARRAILH, J., - WESTMAN, - WAERUM, [Allocution, Discours, Paroles] « Les Pays du Nord à l'Université de Paris. Cinquantenaire du transfert des collections fennoscandinaves de la Bibliothèque Sainte-Geneviève dans son annexe. 5 Novembre 1953 », *Annales de l'Université de Paris*, 24 (1954), 24-39.

WICKERSHEIMER, E., *Dictionnaire biographique des médecins en France au moyen âge*, Paris, 1936.

WIDEEN, H., *Skara domkyrka. Kort historik och vägledning*, Skara, 1953.

INDEX

Barra, J. de, 151.
Barreau, Hector, 116 n.
Barsail. *See* Thomas.
Barthelemy Morel, 105 n.
Basel, Council of, 82 n.
Baudet (Baldeuino) le Flament (Fleming), burgher, 70, 70 n, 74, 120, 155, 156, 172, 174.
Bayeux, bishop of, 33.
Beauvais, College of, 88, 105, 111, 117.
Beckmann, H., 94, 175.
Bedolfe, T., 4, 12.
Bedolfe, W., 4, 12.
Beichner, P. E., 26 n, 175.
Benedictus, bishop of Skara, 69.
Benedictus de Londoniis, 136, 140, 142, 143, 145, 147.
Benedictus (Bengt) Johannis (Johansson), 68.
Benedictus Olavi, 98 n.
Berg, H., 49 n, 51 n, 175.
Bero Gregorii de Suecia, 77 n.
Bertrandi Canatarius. *See* Guillelmus.
Berty, A., 18 n, 30 n, 35, 35 n, 75 n, 116, 117 n.
Biterne (Betourne, Bisterne). *See* Guillelmus.
Blanka, Queen, 61 n.
Blok (Bloc). *See* Guillelmus.
Blondi. *See* Robertus.
Boemundus (Boemond, Bumundus) Theodorici de Lutrea (de Luttre, Kaiserslautern), beadle of the English-German Nation, 41, 42, 87, 87 n, 88 n, 90, 101, 102, 111, 111 n, 113 n.
Boethius, bishop of Växjö († 1291), 49, 49 n.
Boethius, G., 175.
Boetius, bishop of Växjö († 1343), 49 n.
Boniface IX, Pope, 82.
Bonneuil, Etienne, Plate V.
Bonrode. *See* Johannes.
Bons Enfants-d'Arras, College of, 47 n.
Bordeaux, Cathedral, 61.
Bosco. *See* Nicolaus de.
Boyce, G. C., 37 n, 70 n, 175.
Breviarium Scarense, Plate XII.
Briffaut. *See* Petrus.
Brilioth, Y., 52 n, 96 n, 176.

Broequerke (Broghard), Nicolaus de, 68.
Brynulphus (Brynolf) Algotsson, bishop of Skara, 18 n, 51, 51 n, 52, 52 n, 55, 61, 67, 119, 171, 173; seals of, 52, 55, Plates X, XI.
Brynulphus Gerlaksson, bishop of Skara, Plate XII.
Brynulphus (Brunyulphus, Bryniulphe, Brunulphus) Karlsson (Karoli, Charles, Carlsson), provost, later bishop of Skara, 73-77, 84, 89, 111, 119, 157, 171, 173; seals of, 75, 89, Plates XXI, XXIV.
Budinszky, A., 18 n, 73 n, 176.
Bulaeus [Du Boulay], C. E., 18 n, 176.

Cadran (Quadran), Maison du, 20 n, 110, 116, 117, 120, 129, 137, 172, 174; title deeds of, 123.
Caesaris. *See* Petrus.
Calendar of Peter of Dacia, 99 n.
Calmette, G., 12.
Calot (Kalot). *See* Guillelmus.
Campis. *See* Everardus de; Johannes de.
Canatarius. *See* Guillelmus.
Carlsson, G., 99 n, 176.
Carpentarius. *See* Philippus.
Carroll, G. L., 12.
Cauchon. *See* Pierre.
Chatelain, E. (Ae.), 18 n, 20 n, 30 n, 99 n, 176.
Chevalier, [C.] U. [J.], 55 n, 176.
Chevalier au Cygne, printshop, 103 n.
Christensen, W., 82 n, 177.
Christianus (Christiern) Hemmingi (Hemmingsen), bishop of Ribe, 82, 82 n.
Claudin, A., 103 n, 176.
Clivis, Jordanus de, 73.
Colleges. *See* Beauvais; Bons Enfants-d'Arras; Dacia; France; Linköping (*see* Linköping House); Lombards; Scottish Students; Skara (*see* Skara House); Sorbonne; Upsala.
Cologne, University, 41 n, 99 n, 101 n.
Compigne. *See* Johannes de; Pelerin de.
Concasty, M. L., 38 n.
Conradus Henrici, 98 n.
Conradus, illuminator, 55 n, 119, 136, 171, 173.
Conradus Suart, 98 n.

Constance, Council of, 96.
Constancia, daughter of Thierricus, 23.
Corke. *See* Arvidus.
Coustepointier. *See* Robertus le.
Crespin, Master, tenant of Skara House, 115, 115 n.

Daae, L., 77 n, 176.
Dacia. *See* Hermannus de; Michael de; Navno Johannis de.
Dacia, College of, 15, 18, 33, 77.
Dahl, S., 82 n, 177.
Dahlberg, E. J., 17 n, 58 n, 176, Plates II, IV, V, VII, VIII, XIV.
Dahlgren, S., 77 n, 84 n, 181.
Danielis, Johannes, 98 n.
Deflandre, D., 12.
Denifle, H., 18 n, 30 n, 176.
Dentem, Johannes ad, 143.
Derthesen, Jordanus de, 81 n.
Dinteren, Henricus de, 85, 85 n.
Disciplina scholarium, 74.
Dittrich, A., 180.
Dodier, Simon, 116, 116 n.
Doll. *See* Guillelmus.
Domus Dacie, 15, 18, 33, 77.
Dorp. *See* Johannes.
Douaco. *See* Jacobus de.
Du Boulay. *See* Bulaeus.
Du Breul, J., 111 n, 177.
Durandus, 126.

Egidius (de) Jutfaes, 78 n, 80 n.
Eldblom, K., 12.
Emphastus (Anfaste, Hemphastus, Hemfestus, Hemfredus, Erkallus [?]), canon of Växjö, later canon of Skara, 49-71, 74, 81, 110, 119, 120, 134-137, 138, 139, 141, 143, 146, 148, 152, 154, 171-174; seal of, 69, Plate XX.
Engelstoft, 177, 182.
Engelstoft, P., 82 n, 177.
English-German Nation. *See* University of Paris.
Erfurt, University, 41 n.
Erik, Duke, 61 n.
Erik [of Pomerania], King, 82 n.
Erkallus, 156. *See* Emphastus.
Erlandus, canon of Linköping, 35.

Erslev, Kr., 82 n, 177.
Eschildus, student in Paris, 71.
Eskil, archbishop of Lund, 49.
Estienne le Riche, 75, 120, 157, 172, 174.
Etienne Bonneuil, Plate V.
Euardus de Suessia, 68.
Eubel, C., 31 n, 49 n, 67 n, 82 n, 89 n, 91 n, 177.
Everardi de Yselstein, Henricus, 91, 161.
Everardus de Campis, canon and chamberlain of Saint-Marcel, 35.
Everhardi (Everardi) de Swecia, Hermannus, 73, 77 n.

Fabri, Thomas, 82.
Falcdol [Falkdal]. *See* Gotscaldus.
Falköping, 57, 143, 146, 148, Plates XIV, XVI; seal of, 58, Plate XV.
Fant, E. M., 77 n, 91 n, 177, 182.
Fant, G. F., 177.
Felisc (Felize). *See* Pierre.
Fischer, E., 61 n, 177.
Flament. *See* Baudet le; Pierre le.
Flicke, Johannes, 98 n.
Ford, P., 12.
Forestarii, Galterus, 80 n.
Forsell, C. G., Plate XVI.
France, College of, 117, 120, 172.
Franklin, A., 113 n, 177.
Fredericus Traest (to be identified with Fredericus Trask ?), 84 n.
Fredericus Trask (Traest [?]), canon of Åbo, 40.
Frees, Henricus, 98 n.
Frille. *See* Haquinus.

Gabriel, A. L., 26 n, 177, 178.
Galle, Petrus Johannis, 99 n.
Gallén, J., 177.
Gallot, Antoine, 117 n.
Galterus Forestarii, 80 n.
Gams, P. B., 49 n, 82 n.
Gandilhon, R., 75 n, 178.
Garsonnet, Jehan, 116 n.
Garvin, J. N., 11, 178.
Geffroy, A., 29 n, 30 n, 178.
Geijer, E. G., 51 n, 99 n.
Georgius, proctor of Linköping House, 41.
Georgius Rain, 78 n.

Gerardus de Kalkar, 73.

Géraud, H., 23 n, 55 n, 109 n, 178.

German Students, House of, 15.

Gille Haquin, provost of Paris, 155.

Gilson, E., 36 n, 178.

Glane, Jacques, 116.

Glorieux, P., 26 n, 178.

Godscalcus Witte, 98 n.

Gortenbeke. See Johannes de.

Goswinus (Gossuinus, Goussoin) Schopenhagel (Schuppenaghel, Schuppennagel, Schopenagel), beadle, 102-105, 115, 116.

Gotscaldus [Gotskalk] Falcdol [Falkdal], bishop of Linköping, 36.

Graffardi. See Thomas.

Grandes-Ecoles-de-Droit (Grand Décret, School of Canon Law), 102, 105, 111, 113, 116, 120, 172, 174.

Gregorii de Suecia, Bero, 77 n.

Gregorius, bishop of Växjö, 49 n.

Gregorius Haffnerlande, 98 n.

Gregory XII, Pope, 84.

Greifswald, University, 41 n.

Gristanus de Suessia, 68.

Grotte. See Sven.

Guberstat. See Johannes.

Gudmar Magnusson, 67-68.

Guérard, M., 47 n, 178.

Guesnon, A., 47 n, 178.

Guiardus de Latigniaco, 120, 138, 172, 174.

Guido de Svecio, 71.

Guillaume Malicorne (Malicornensis), 164.

Guillebertus (Gillebertus, Gilebertus) de Volta (Voute, Vouta), 45 n, 47, 119, 125, 143, 150, 171, 173.

Guillelmus (Guillermus), archdeacon, Officialis, 45, 125, 127, 130.

Guillelmus Bertrandi Canatarius (Canetier), 55, 65, 67, 70 n, 120, 134, 135, 150, 151, 172, 174.

Guillelmus (Guillermus, Guillaume) Biterne (Betourne, Bisterne), beadle, 45, 47, 70 n, 109, 110, 119, 125, 127, 130-132, 134, 138, 141, 143, 150, 152, 154, 171, 173.

Guillelmus (Wilhelmus) Blok (Bloc), tenant of Linköping House, 37, 85 n.

Guillelmus Calot (Kalot), 63, 110, 119, 134, 141, 146, 171, 173.

Guillelmus de Orvalle (Orval), son-in-law of Guillelmus Biterne, beadle, 47, 49, 57, 119, 130-133, 134, 138, 141, 143, 171, 173.

Guillelmus Doll, owner of House Ad Cornu Cervi, 36.

Gunno (Gunne) Andree (Andersson) Prika, canon of Skara, 91, 161.

Gyllensten, I., 12.

Gyrsting. See Jens.

Haarlem. See Jacobus de.

Haffnerlande, Gregorius, 98 n.

Hagues, Pierre, 102 n.

Håkan Magnusson, 52.

Hallberg, S., 12.

Haquin. See Gille.

Haquini de Orabro, Thomas, 71 n.

Haquinus Andree, seu Frille, 98 n.

Haraldus, canon of Linköping, 35.

Hartikim, Laurentius, 98 n.

Hébert, M., 178.

Hector Barreau, 116 n.

Hemingus, canon of Upsala, 29.

Hemming, 91 n.

Hemmingi (Hemmingsen). See Christianus.

Henninghus Rocstede, Paris scholar, 91, 161.

Henricus Andree de Svecia, 77 n.

Henricus de Dinteren, 85.

Henricus de Suessia, 68, 68 n.

Henricus Everardi de Yselstein, 91, 161.

Henricus Frees, 98 n.

Henricus Kanuti, 98 n.

Henricus Ludwigsson, canon of Upsala, 30.

Henricus Magni de Suecia, 77 n.

Henricus Nicolai, 98 n.

Henricus Nicolai de Svecia, 98 n.

Henrici, Conradus, 98 n.

Henry Alexandre, 115.

Hermanni (Hermensson). See Nicolaus.

Hermannus de Dacia, 84.

Hermannus Everhardi (Everardi) de Swecia, 73, 77 n.

Hermelin, S. G., Plate XVI.

Hildebrand, E., 176.

Hildebrand, H., 17 n, 61 n, 178.

Hildebrandi, Johannes, 40.
Hillairet, J., 178.
Hjelmstjerne, 182.
Hoffbauer, F., 178, Plate I.
Hofmeister, A., 101 n, 178.
Holma, H., 98 n, 178.
Holmquist, H., 176.
Holt, Severinus, 98 n.
Holy Thorn, the, 52.
Honorius III, Pope, 61.
Hotel du Chatel, a house, 113 n.
Hours of the Blessed Virgin, 26.
Houses. *See* Cadran; *Domus Dacie;* German Students; *Hotel du Chatel;* Linköping *(ad Cornu Cervi); Pomi Rubei;* Saint-Michel; Skara *(ad Imaginem Nostre Domine).*
Hugnin, Al. Fr., 179.
Hure. *See* Jacobus.

Imperio. *See* Oliverus de.
Illuminator. *See* Conradus.
Ingeborg Knutsdotter, 89 n.
Ingeldus Jonsson, clerk, 30.
Inghen, Marsilius de, 36.
Ingimarus, Master, 30.
Ingolphus Olavi, 99 n.
Ingrid Karlsdotter, 89 n.
Ioenen [?], Richardus, 37.
Isabellis (Ysabellis), daughter of Guillelmus Biterne, 47, 130.

Jacobi, Arvidus, 98 n.
Jacobus, archbishop of Upsala, 23.
Jacobus de Douaco (Duaco), 111 n, 119, 146, 171, 173.
Jacobus Hure, son-in-law of Guillelmus Biterne, 47, 131-133.
Jacobus Johannis de Haarlem, 84, 87, 90.
Jacobus Petri de Roda, 98 n.
Jacobus Ulfonisk, 99 n.
Jacobus Winthorst de Hamburg (Hamborch), 101.
Jacques Glane, 116.
Jägersköld, O., 12.
Jaillot, J. B. M., 29 n, 109 n, 110 n, 179.
Jehan. *See* Johannes.
Jehan, Master, owner of a house, 115.
Jehan Garsonnet, 116 n.

Jehan le Maistre, pittancer of Sainte-Geneviève, 116 n.
Jehan Missart, 116.
Jehan Noël, 75, 157.
Jehanne. *See* Johanna.
Jehanne, daughter of Guillelmus Calot, 70 n.
Jens Gyrsting, judge, 82 n.
Jessen, F. v., 179.
Johanna, daughter of Guillelmus Biterne, 47, 131-133.
Johanna, wife of Guillelmus Biterne, 45, 47, 119, 127, 130, 132, 171, 173.
Johanna (Jehanne), wife of Michael de Sancta-Susanna, 65, 67, 120, 150, 152, 172, 174.
Johanna, wife of Robertus le Coustepointier, 57, 119, 138, 171, 173.
Johanna de Archiis, 120, 138, 172, 174.
Johannes, archdeacon of Linköping, 35.
Johannes, priest, 68, 70 n.
Johannes ad Dentem, 143.
Johannes Adolphi, archbishop of Upsala, 25, 51.
Johannes Bonrode, tenant of Linköping House, 36.
Johannes Danielis, 98 n.
Johannes de Campis, 55, 120, 134, 135, 172, 174.
Johannes (Jehan) de Compigne, 70, 155.
Johannes de Gortenbeke, doctor decretorum, 36.
Johannes de Linköping, 68, 70 n.
Johannes de Suecia, 29.
Johannes de Volta (Voute, Vouta), son of Guillebertus de Volta, 47, 120, 125, 126, 172, 173.
Johannes Dorp, tenant of Linköping House, 37.
Johannes Flicke, 98 n.
Johannes Guberstat, notary public, 40.
Johannes Hildebrandi, 40.
Johannes Langh de Arusia, 98 n.
Johannes Luberti, 73.
Johannes Magni, 98 n.
Johannes Mullinger de Austria, 80 n.
Johannes Nicolai de Suessia, 68.
Johannes Olavi de Svecia, bishop of Åbo, 98 n.

Johannes Pauli, 98 n.
Johannes Penneser, owner of a house, 42.
Johannes Petri, 98 n.
Johannes Picard, tenant of Linköping House, 37.
Johannes Tungern, 81 n.
Johannis (Johansson). *See* Benedictus.
Johannis (Krigebusk) de Dacia. *See* Navno.
Johannis de Haarlem. *See* Jacobus.
Johannis de Swecia, Andreas, 77 n.
Johannis Galle, Petrus, 99 n.
Johansson, H., 55 n, 179.
John Stoll, 103 n.
Johnsen, A. O., 179.
Jonsson. *See* Ingeldus.
Jordanus de Clivis, 73.
Jordanus de Derthesen, 81 n.
Jørgensen, E., 68 n, 82 n, 179.
Jutfaes, Egidius (de), 78 n, 80 n.

Kalkar, Gerardus de, 73.
Kanuti, Henricus, 98 n.
Kanutus, bishop of Linköping, 40, 41.
Karl (Karolus) Uddsson (Udsons, Udonis), dean of Skara, 90 n, 98; seal of, 98 n, Plate XXVII.
Karlsdotter, Ingrid, 89 n.
Karlsson (Karoli). *See* Brynulphus.
Karlsson, K. H., 81 n, 99 n, 179.
Kellerman, G., 179.
Keussen, H., 99 n, 101 n, 179.
Kibre, P., 70 n, 179.
Knutsdotter, Ingeborg, 89 n.
Kohler, Ch., 75 n, 179.
Kumlien, K., 18 n, 68 n, 180.

Lagaböter : *See* Magnus.
l'Alemant. *See* Simon.
Langebek, J., 82 n, 99 n, 180, 182.
Langh, Johannes — de Arusia, 98 n.
Lanhers, Y., 12.
La Palmière, a house, 110, 148.
Latigniaco. *See* Guiardus de.
Laurencii de Suecia, Nicolaus, 68.
Laurencius Olavi de Thuna, canon of Upsala, student in Paris, 42, 99 n.
Laurentii, alias Monachi, Andreas, 98 n.
Laurentius Albani de Suessia, 68.
Laurentius de Suessia, 68.

Laurentius de Upsalia, 68.
Laurentius Hartikim, 98 n.
Laurentius Michaelis Suurpae, bishop of Åbo, 98 n.
Laurentius Olavi, archdeacon of Vesterås, 42 n.
Laurentius Olavi, canon of Upsala, 42 n.
Laurentius Rannaldi, 98 n.
Laurentius Sturberin de Suessia, 68.
Lazenby, F., 12.
Lebeuf, J., 109 n, 180.
Leipzig, University, 41 n.
Liebman, Ch., Plate XXX.
Liljegren, J. G., 23 n, 180.
Linguonis, Paulis, 98 n.
Linköping, Johannes de, 68, 70 n.
Linköping :
 bishops, 36, 40, 41.
 cathedral, Plate VII.
 Cathedral Chapter, 35, 37, 40, 41, 96 n.
 diocese, 33, 36.
Linköping House, 15, 18, 33, 35-43, 77, 96 n, Plate I.
Lobineau, G., 18 n, 177.
Lombards, College of, 35.
Londoniis. *See* Benedictus de.
Longnon, M. A., 180.
Louvain, University, 41 n.
Lübeck, Radulphus de, 74.
Luberti, Johannes, 73.
Luca. *See* Petrus de.
Ludwigsson. *See* Henricus.
Lund, 49, 82 n.
Lundholm, K. G., 89 n, 180.
Lundquist, B., 57 n.
Lutrea. *See* Boemundus Theodorici de.

Maerscalli, Thomas, 37.
Magni. *See* Johannes; Olavus.
Magni de Suecia, Henricus, 77 n.
Magnus, bishop of Växjö, 49.
Magnus, King, 61 n.
Magnus Lagaböter, King, 52.
Magnus Nicolai Särkiläx, bishop of Åbo, 98 n.
Magnusson : Gudmar, 67-68; Håkan, 52.
Mahieu, B., 12.
Maillez. *See* Arnulphus as.
Maistre. *See* Jehan le.

190

193

123, 137, 171-174, Plates XXVIII, XXIX, XXX;

Rue Josselin (Jocelin, *ruella Jocelini Anglici, vicus Jocellini*, later Bouvard), 35, 65, 110, 119, 129, 134, 148, 150, 171, 173;

Rue Saint-Hilaire (Rue du-Mont-Saint-Hilaire, *vicus Sancti Illarii*, Rue Fromentel), 35, 40, 42, 71, 75, 113, 117, 119, 157, 171, 173;

Rue Serpente, 23, 25, 29, 31.

Sturberin, Laurentius — de Suessia, 68.

Suart, Conradus, 98 n.

Sueno, proctor of Emphastus, 67-70, 73, 119, 152, 154.

Suessia (Suecia, Swecia, Svecia, Svecio). *See* Andreas Johannis de, Bero Gregorii de, Euardus de, Gristanus de, Guido de, Henricus de, Henricus Andree de, Henricus Magni de, Henricus Nicolai de, Hermannus Everhardi de, Johannes Nicolai de, Johannes Olavi de, Laurentius de, Laurentius Albani de, Laurentius Sturberin de, Nicolaus de, Nicolaus Laurentius de, Oliverus de, Philippus de, Ruthgerus Trost de, Thomas de.

Suhm, P. F., 82 n, 99 n, 180, 182.

Sunaman, martyr, nephew of Saint Sigfrid, 51, 51 n.

Suurpae. *See* Laurentius Michaelis.

Svalenius, I., 49 n, 51 n, 175.

Sven Grotte, bishop of Skara, 84 n.

Swensson, H., 182.

Tavern, *Ad habitum Gilleti*, 74.

Tesson. *See* Richardus.

Theodorici de Lutrea. *See* Boemundus.

Thierricus (Thendonis), 23.

Thirion, J., 178.

Thomas Barsail (Bursail), 57, 119, 138, 171, 173.

Thomas de Suecia, 71 n.

Thomas de Tyha, *clericus*, son-in-law of Guillelmus Biterne, 47, 130.

Thomas Fabri, 82.

Thomas Graffardi, 31.

Thomas Haquini de Orabro, 71 n.

Thomas Maerscalli, 37.

Thomassia, daughter of Guillelmus Biter-

ne, 47, 49, 119, 133-134, 136, 141, 143, 171, 173.

Thornqvist, C., 183.

Thorstanus of Olandia, 68.

Thuna. *See* Laurencius Olavi de.

Thurot, C., 70 n, 183.

Tierri l'Alemant, 23 n.

Tisserand, L. M., 18 n, 175.

Toulouse, M., 183.

Traest. *See* Fredericus.

Trask. *See* Fredericus.

Trost, Ruthgerus — de Swecia, 79, 82 n.

Tungern, Johannes, 81 n.

Tyha. *See* Thomas de.

Tyrrerus, visitor in Paris, 91 n.

Udd Matsson, 89 n.

Uddsson (Odonis, Otson, Odzssons). *See* Karl; Mats; Siggo.

Ulfonisk, Jacobus, 99 n.

Unaman, martyr, nephew of Saint Sigfrid, 51, 51 n.

University of Paris, 18 n, 25, 33, 47, 49 n, 51, 70, 77, 80, 105;

English-German Nation, 15-20, 30-33, 36-43, 70-75, 79-91, 96, 99, 101-105, 113-117, 120, 136, 137, 162, 164, 172, 174;

beadles, 41, 42, 87 n, 101;

calendar of, 99;

chartulary, 113;

inventory of properties, 33, 40 n, 88 n;

officers, 17, 18, 82 n, 84 n, 101 n, 105, 162, 164;

students,

Danish, 18;

Swedish, 17, 18, 29, 31, 33, 36, 37, 67, 68, 71, 77, 78, 79, 84-88, 90, 98, 101, 110 n, 119, 171, 173;

title deeds of properties, 123;

Faculty of Arts, 41, 45;

Faculty of Law, 90;

Faculty of Theology, 57 n;

French Nation, 45;

Schools. *See* Grandes-Ecoles-de-Droit; Petites-Ecoles-de-Décret.

Upsala, Plate IV;

archbishops, 23, 25, 29, 30, 51;

cathedral, Plate V;

194

Cathedral Chapter, 23, 25, 29, 30;
Cathedral School, 23, 25;
College of, in Paris, 15, 26-29, 33, 35,
   Plates I, VI;
     statutes, 25-29, 51, 90;
     diocese, 25, 29, 51, 98;
     province of, 31;
     Universitetsbibliotek, 167.
Upsalia, Laurentius de, 68.

Vallée, L., 113 n, 183.
Valous, [G.] de, 183.
Van Moé, Ae. A., 20 n, 182.
Västergötland, 52, Plate XXIII.
Växjö :
   bishops, 49;
   Cathedral Chapter, 49; seal of, 49, 51,
   Plate IX;
   Church of, 49;
   Church of Saint Olof, 57 n;
   city, 49, Plate VIII; seal of, Plate XIII.
Vernet, Mme A., 12.
Vesterås, 82 n, 98.
Vielliard, J., 12.

Vienna, University, 41 n.
Villa Blovana, Petrus de, 110, 134.
Vinaman, martyr, nephew of Saint Sig-
   frid, 51, 51 n.
Volta (Voute, Vouta). *See* Guillebertus
   de; Johannes de.
Vos, Nicholaus, 105.

Waerum, 183.
Wagner. *See* Petrus Caesaris.
Waldemar, Duke, 61 n.
Werlauff, E. C., 182.
Westman, 183.
Wickersheimer, E., 31 n, 183.
Wideen, H., 67 n, 183.
Wilhelmus Bloc. *See* Guillelmus.
William Pelterer *(pelliparius)*, 23.
Winandus, provost of the Cathedral of
   Åbo, 36.
Winthorst, Jacobus — de Hamburg, 101.
Witte, Godscalcus, 98 n.

Yselstein, Henricus Everardi de, 91, 161.

With ecclesiastical permission. October 9, 1960.

TEXTS AND STUDIES
IN THE HISTORY OF MEDIAEVAL EDUCATION

EDITED BY A. L. GABRIEL AND J. N. GARVIN

Printed in Belgium